APPROACHING GOD

APPROACHING GOD

Lisa Repko Borden

**MONARCH
BOOKS**

OXFORD, UK & GRAND RAPIDS, MICHIGAN, USA

First published in the UK in 2010 by Monarch Books
(a publishing imprint of Lion Hudson plc),
Wilkinson House, Jordan Hill Road, Oxford OX2 8DR.
Tel: +44 (0)1865 302750 Fax: +44 (0)1865 302757
Email: monarch@lionhudson.com
www.lionhudson.com

ISBN: 978-1-85424-948-7

Reprinted 2010.

Distributed by:
UK: Marston Book Services Ltd, PO Box 269, Abingdon, Oxon OX14 4YN;
USA: Kregel Publications, PO Box 2607, Grand Rapids, Michigan 49501

Photographs courtesy of: pp. 63, 91, 99, 128, 138, 153, 154 Bill Bain; p. 130 Gerry Bessent; pp. 21, 26–27, 150 Jesse Borden; pp. 31, 35, 36–37, 117, 135 Lisa Borden; pp. 109, 124 Trevor Borden; pp. 7, 79, 85, 105, 107 Roger Chouler; pp. 45, 54, 61, 82 Corbis; pp. 65, 73 Steve Denler; pp. 100, 143, 156 Andrew King; pp. 23, 43, 51, 121 Estelle Lobban; p. 127 Geoff Nobes; pp. 103, 131, 137, 141, 145 Joel Phillips; p. 112 Peter Russell; pp. 87, 94 Skyler Russell; p. 40 Jeff Shipley; p. 59 Kathryn Smith; p. 149 Suzanne Tietjen.

British Library Cataloguing Data
A catalogue record for this book is available from the British Library.

Printed and bound in the USA.

For Byron
and our children,
Jesse, Trevor, Colin and Heather,
who teach me every day how to
know and love God.

And for Haley,
because, when we were thirteen,
I promised.

Contents

Acknowledgments

Many thanks are due…

… to Stephanie Heald for pursuing and encouraging me.

… to Tony Collins for taking a chance and for helping me along.

… to Tait Davidson for frequent cheerful text messages.

… to Maureen Hurst for hours spent in careful reading and for many helpful comments.

… to Sue Klein for exuberant support.

… to Dana Dusbiber for love and inspiration.

… to Peter, Tammy, Skyler, Chase, Sianna and Leighton Russell for being family.

… to Nelly D'Alessandro for extraordinary friendship.

… to my sister, Tanya Randall, for a bond that crosses oceans.

… to my kids, who have always told their mama to write.

… and mostly to Byron, who never doubted for a second.

Foreword

I think it was that gnarly old sage A. W. Tozer who said that the most important thing about any one of us is the very first thing that comes into our minds when we hear the word "God". That being so, this exquisite little book leads us deeper into the most important discovery of our lives: a fuller, more familiar, encounter with God.

Whisper that three-letter word to Lisa Borden and she hears wonderful associations such as "friend", "father", "mother", "healer", "guide" and even "artist". She approaches God with confidence and joy. What a contrast this is with so many of my friends, who tag God's name with judgmentalism, male chauvinism, religious terrorism, boredom or, merely, tragically with irrelevance. In such a context the epiphanies of love celebrated in *Approaching God* are as radical as they are refreshing. Tozer understood that if we misunderstand God we will misunderstand everything else in life. For instance, if we consider God cruel and uncaring, our reflex reactions are likely to be fuelled by fear and a desire to control. Similarly, if we doubt God's existence, we will probably be driven by an existential urge to accumulate selfish experiences in order to impose meaning upon the apparent absurdity and pointlessness of life. But if we allow the reality of God's love – depicted so beautifully in this book – to seep osmotically into our subconscious, then we will become increasingly kind, creative and prayerful.

No fewer than thirty-five times the psalmist says of God that "His love endures for ever". The fourteenth-century anchorite nun Julian of Norwich, who endured her fair share of suffering, reflected on the implications of such unquenchable love and concluded simply that "all shall be well, and all shall be well, and all manner of things shall be well". At the heart of Lisa Borden's message is an ancient certainty that God's love is constantly bubbling up and breaking through in the very simplest stuff of life, even the darkness and pain. Since, as the apostle Paul writes, "we know that in all things God works for the good of those who love him" (Romans 8:28), the greatest surprise in the long litany of tears that makes up human history will surely be (and I can imagine a heavenly drum-roll even as I dare to type the words) that *ultimately everything is going to be OK*.

I have the joy of knowing Lisa well, although I never knew just how beautifully she could write until now. She is my friend, and together we're caught up in a global community of people seeking to live at the intersection of prayer, mission and justice. We have often laughed and talked together, and she really does live the stuff that she writes about in this book. She became a missionary (I bet she hates that word!) and kissed the American dream goodbye in order to raise her family on three separate continents. Her insights have therefore been enriched by many cultures, not least that of Tanzania, where she wrote this book, and her faith has been tempered by faithfulness over many years. Lisa has come to reflect so many of the characteristics of God explored in this book (and she'll *definitely* hate me saying this bit!): she's a wise guide to many, a kind friend, a quiet healer, a good parent and, yes, as you'll see, she's an artist too.

Speaking of parents, I especially love Lisa's chapter about God as Mother. This oft-forgotten biblical aspect of divinity is, I believe, an essential key to unlock the good news of the gospel for so many people who have been damaged, deserted or just plain disappointed by their human fathers.

Maybe it makes sense to conclude with a simple prayer of approach:

Lord Jesus, may we approach You through the thoughts and the words in this book. Open our eyes to read between the lines, that we may approach Your world with new grace. Open our ears to new vocabulary, that we may approach our neighbours with words that heal. And open our hearts to be surprised, relieved and changed by the old, old gospel of your love, that we may even approach ourselves with the message of salvation. Amen.

Pete Greig
Guildford, England
www.24-7prayer.com

without ceasing

and this is how we pray
backs nestled into the hammock
faces turned toward the stars
the warm air lifts against us
and we are quiet, quiet
as you, God, speak to us
about how big you are

and this is how we pray
sitting on the leaf-strewn ground
peering across the pattern of sun and shade
to the clear pool under the giant fig
where the monitor lizard slips through the water
and we whisper our worshipful thanks
again and again

and this is how we pray
standing in the kitchen
speaking out the worries in our minds
telling this perfect parent God
just how small our faith feels
conscious of how sweetly ludicrous
our doubts must appear

and this is how we pray
curled into our duvets
safely tucked in on this wind-blown night
thoughts far from here
with our friends who sit in vigil
waiting for a precious life to pass
maybe even tonight

and this is how we pray
with longing
and with hope
with stress
and with joy
with daring
and with simple words

God as Friend...

after you left

stone-cold heart
hard-pressed
tomb-still

i stand here
knowing only
that they killed you
then stole my chance
to wrap you
in the sweetness
you deserve

a gardener's voice
breaks into the emptiness
i hear my answer
from across a thousand miles
of loneliness

mary
he says
mary

my dead heart
startles

and chokes
awake

this vacant place
that was my chest
rushes warmth

mary

a creator's power
invoking life
where there had been none

mary

and i knew you
i knew you

by the way
you said
my name

God as Friend

(Good Company)

It was a morning of multi-tasking through domestic and professional duties. The normal list of laundry and shopping, answering work-related emails and trying to prepare a presentation pushed me along, as I responded to my children and arranged for colleagues to come to dinner. As the lunch hour rolled around, I went to grab something quickly, intending to eat as I stood at my kitchen counter and continued with my work.

Through the vague background noise of the list still humming in my head, I heard a simple question.

"Where are you?"

I recognized the voice; the question put so simply. Long ago, God called out to his new friends, Adam and Eve, wondering where they were. Gazing out my window, I imagined that scene so distant from my own world.

The garden is cool and dewy as the shadows begin to stretch across the tender new grass. All the colors change, as the sun slides down the sky and begins to take its leave for the day. Here, in the shifting light of each evening, a small group of friends enjoy the simple pleasure of conversation – the richness of life shared – as they talk together under the canopy of trees.

I am seeing the picture painted in the earliest verses of the Bible, sparked by the briefest mention of God stopping by in the evening to visit with Adam and Eve. He dropped in on His friends. To walk... to talk... to be with them. For all its beauty, this simple picture of friendship is the backdrop to a call of longing and a deep sense of loss.

The picture unfolds.

The man and his wife heard the sound of the Lord God walking in the garden in the cool of the day... They hid from him... And God called to them, "Where are you?"

"Where are you?"

One of God's first questions to humankind is "Where are you?"

Slipped between the Creation story right at the beginning of the Bible and the next big event (the loss of paradise that came as a result of human failure), this subtle revelation of God tells us so much about His desire for our relationship with Him. Easy to miss between the larger events that bracket it, this picture of God coming into the garden and looking for His friends tells us that God was and is longing for our friendship – a friendship that we have pulled back from.

Despite many man-made portraits of God and His relationship toward us since then, we can't get around the fact that this biblical image of God seeking us portrays His longing for *friendship with us*. While God is far and away the most powerful party in the trio we find in the Genesis account, He has not stipulated that Adam and Eve keep a respectful distance from Him. Instead, God shows up every evening to catch up with His two new companions. As the cool begins to usher in the evening, God and His friends like to go for a meander.

This revealing glimpse in Genesis of God's heart for friendship with His children is not the only place in Scripture where we see His desire. Different biblical characters along the way confirm, through their own relationship with God, this intention He has.

Abraham is remembered for many things. He dared to believe God's wild promises and followed the prompting he felt to leave his homeland and go to "a place that God would show him". God had made a promise to him regarding a large family that would grow into a large nation, thus blessing the entire earth. This rather big promise was particularly poignant because Abraham's wife, Sarah, was not able to have children. The two of them were getting older and the promise was, by all measures, outrageous.

27

And yet, Abraham believed. He believed and he ventured out into unknown territory, because he chose to trust God's prompting and believe that God would somehow fulfill His word to him.

Many hundreds of years later, James, a New Testament writer, refers to Abraham as a *friend of God*. James 2:23 says:

> *"Abraham believed God, and it was credited to him*
> *as righteousness," and he was called God's friend.*

It was God Himself who first called Abraham His friend, back in the Old Testament book of Isaiah. Abraham trusted and believed and God called him "friend".

David, the poet king, is another one who lived in friendship with God. I believe one of the truest marks of real friendship is when we share our deepest self with that other person. No holds barred: the real me in all my yuck and glory. This is how David related to God. His poetry, the Psalms, taught the nation of Israel that God was intimately concerned with the things on their minds. David complains bitterly, loves expressively, and confides easily to God in all his writings. Consider Psalm 13:

> *How long, O Lord? Will you forget me forever?*
> *How long will you hide your face from me?*
> *How long must I wrestle with my thoughts*
> *and day after day have sorrow in my heart?*

How long will my enemy triumph over me?
Look on me and answer, Lord my God.
Give light to my eyes, or I will sleep in death;
my enemy will say, "I have overcome him,"
and my foes will rejoice when I fall.
But I trust in your unfailing love;
my heart rejoices in your salvation.
I will sing the Lord's praise,
for he has been good to me.

Quite an array of emotions is exposed in David's rant! When the time came for a new king to be appointed over Israel, the Old Testament says that God was searching for "a man after his own heart". In this search, He directed the prophet Samuel to the young shepherd David. David, for all his passion and promise, future failures and victories, was that man after the heart of God. He was a true friend who would bare his inmost thoughts to God, candidly and without reservation.

Jesus also demonstrated friendship with us. Not only did He model intimate friendship in His relationship with John, called "the disciple whom Jesus loved", but He extended His friendship toward all who believe. John 15:15 says:

I no longer call you servants, because servants do not
know their master's business. Instead, I have called
you friends, for everything that I learned from my
Father I have made known to you.

This confiding is not a one-way thing – our confiding in God. Rather, God confides in us as well. Psalm 25:14 says, "The Lord confides in those who fear him; he makes his covenant known to them."

The intention of God for friendship with us is clear throughout the Bible. Yet we seem to pull back from His move toward us. Why?

God as good company; God as friend. Maybe I pull back from relationship with Him because this is not naturally my first impression of God?

To be honest, there is something close to fear that comes up in some of us if we dare relax into this image of God. Are we really allowed to think of this Awesome Presence, this Ultimate Life, this Vast Hugeness and Perfect Love, as "friend"? Is it low, disrespectful or outrageous of us to think that this Tremendous Being would want to know us and be known by us?

Yet in the many accounts of Scripture we find God pursuing the company of humanity. As overwhelming and even slightly awkward as it might seem, we need to accept what this is telling us. God wants to be with us. He wants us to be with Him.

My own friendship with God began in childhood. Looking back, I can see that my parents modeled something accessibly simple and friend-like in their relationships with God. They spoke of God as if He were a normal part of everyday life; an expected presence in our home. God didn't seem far away or difficult to reach, with my mom frequently addressing Him in the course of regular conversation.

"Well, Lord, we just ask that you would help us with that!" she might say aloud, as if God was standing in the kitchen with us.

My father continually invited us to approach God with him about any issue at hand. "OK, little team!" he would say, calling us all into their room. The six of us would gather on

the big bed and listen as he described the situation that he felt needed prayer. Perhaps we were due for a holiday but couldn't quite afford one. Perhaps he was going to be away with his work and he wanted us all to be safe and happy during the separation. There was nothing too big or too small, really, to speak to God about.

With their easy sense of God's immediate presence and willing ear, my parents conveyed to us without contrived lessons that God engages in relationship with us and, like any real friend, cares about the normal ups and downs of family life. I don't think they ever doubted that this was an appropriate message to instill in their children, but I'm quite sure their faith in it was put to the test at least once.

As kids, we loved our hamster and we especially enjoyed taking her out to the sandbox with us. She seemed to bask in the freedom of a great big area to play in and we would busy ourselves making hills and valleys and tunnels for her to navigate. It was a hamster haven within safe confines under our watchful eyes.

But one day an adult friend stopped by unexpectedly and we all left the sandbox to go and greet her. We must have all really liked this person, because we were distracted from the building of the great Hamsterville long enough for little Miss Hamster to escape. Returning to the sandbox, we realized with horror that our hamster had blazed a trail out of there and we looked in deep dismay toward the little forest that ran behind our unfenced back garden. This was a disaster bigger than anything any of us had experienced before. This was personal tragedy of the greatest proportions.

My poor mother must have sized up this situation and wondered how on earth she was going to explain the problem of pain and unanswered prayer to her four sobered offspring. And she was going to have to do it alone. My father was away for some weeks, and the job of leading us through the impending crisis of loss and grief couldn't have looked very easy to her.

Somewhere in her heart, my mother felt the courage to pray the impossible prayer with us that we would find our hamster. Emboldened by her example, we began feverishly bombarding God with requests that our tiny pet would be rescued from the big wood. Never mind that there were dogs and cats that roamed freely in the area. Never mind that there were things in the forest that would be happy to eat a small, domesticated rodent. Never mind that this hamster knew nothing about surviving in the real world.

We prayed and, sick at heart, I'm sure, my mother called my dad on another continent and told him to pray. His heart sank too, but he asked his friends to join them in our outrageous request. They prayed fervently, not so much because all these adults were concerned about a little hamster lost in the wood. Rather, the whole thing was about children who were speaking to God about something that mattered a great deal to them. Would God, like a true friend, care about the things that mattered to us? We were too young to be worried about a big question like that, but I know that the importance of our prayers was not lost on our parents. We just assumed that God could be approached as a friend who listens to and cares about what is bothering us. But the job of explaining an outcome contrary to what we were all hoping for would fall to our folks.

As it turned out, the little hamster adapted to her forest life and lived three wild days on the lam. We found her one afternoon, when we noticed the leaves of a fern wiggling just a few feet beyond the boundary of our garden. We moved her back into her cage, where she emptied her storage cheeks of leaves and bugs that she had gathered out there in the big world.

God is not held hostage by prayer – even the prayers of earnest little children. We don't force His hand by making requests; but what I learned as a child is that God is willing and eager to be related to as a friend. He wants to be close, and part of that will always include hearing what is weighing on our minds. In this situation, He allowed four little kids – and quite a few astonished adults – to see His caring heart in practical action. God showed us that He is powerfully able to answer prayer, and I'm not sure that lesson would have sunk in if it hadn't come in the form of His caring friendship toward us that said, "I can help you find your hamster."

What are the implications of God's desire for friendship with us? I think the first one is that there should be no fear in us as we approach God.

Let me digress for a moment and say that by "fear" I don't

mean that healthy respect and acknowledgment of who this being really is that we are approaching. "Fear", in the case of "The fear of the Lord is the beginning of knowledge" (Proverbs 1:7), is this kind of recognition. This "fear" is to know the truth that God is other than us – to concede that we are not God's peers. Though God may dwell within us, we are not God, nor are we equal to God.

When I say that there should be no fear as we approach God, I mean that there should be no cowering, no awful terror, no deeply seated mistrust. These things are not present in any of our authentic human friendships and they need not be present in our relationship with God. Fear is the very thing that pushed Adam and Eve into hiding when God came round for a visit.

They had disobeyed a clear instruction and now they were fearful to be with Him. Of course, the nature of being God meant that He already knew what was going on; and yet He was seeking them out. Their wrong assumption that He was now going to reject them paved the way for fear, which then stopped them from approaching Him.

I know I have done the same. When, in my own stubbornness or misguided notions, I have acted in ways that I knew didn't please God, I've found myself awkward and resistant in our relationship. It's the same in human relationships. When I've said or done something to hurt a friend, I am not always incredibly eager to get together with that person again. I can't help but fear that what happened will somehow leave a scar on our relationship that will never really heal. And in a human relationship that may well be the case. But I must hold onto the truth that, no matter what I may or may not have done, God is still actively looking to keep our relationship alive. He knows me through and through, yet pursues me nonetheless.

As we've already seen, the pursuit that we first described in the garden carries through the Bible to the end. And this leads me to conclude that the pursuit is still on today. The ultimate pursuit, of course, came in the person of Jesus. Philippians 2:6–7 tells us that Jesus was "in very nature" God, but that this status was not clutched onto. Instead, He became a servant and took on the nature of a man.

And why did He do this? *Jesus appeared among us to bridge the separation between the divine and human.* God became a man as an act of pursuit. When you think about it, it was a wildly romantic thing to do. Filled with love for His Creation and frustrated by the gulf now stretching between Him and His children, God went to extreme lengths to open a way for us to know each other again, the way we did in the early days of the garden.

This is the act of someone desperate to engage in relationship. This Supreme Being is, in all sincerity, the Ultimate Friend who goes to disproportionately large efforts to initiate and sustain a friendship with us.

As we realize that there is no need for fear, we are changed in our approach to the Divine. We can come with boldness into the presence of Creator God. Yet boldness is not the same as brashness. This boldness is, rather, a confidence. We may approach with confidence because we know the Supreme One would like to see us. We are not going to be bounced by the Heavenly Host, whoever they are. We have a pass.

Armed with this boldness, what do we now confidently expect? We can expect that God is available and approachable: yes. But, more than this, we can expect that this truth that God desires our company means something quite huge. God desires our company because *He enjoys our friendship.*

When I think of relationships that I enjoy, I find it's a

narrow line of distinction between what aspect of this relationship I am enjoying. Am I simply enjoying the person for who he or she is, or am I enjoying the relationship with this person? In truth, it is entirely both that brings me satisfaction and pleasure. And this leads

me to the realization that revolutionizes how I envision God: God enjoys relationship in general, yes; but, specifically, God enjoys relationship *with me*.

Reflexively, the truth that God enjoys me releases a whole new depth into my relationship with God. I *enjoy* God.

I enjoy God. I like the friendship we share. I am thankful for simple times of just being aware of His presence. Yes, God enjoys us, and we now enjoy Him in return.

What this means is that we are no longer limited to a certain set of circumstances for communication or study, but we are freed into mutual companionship, as well. While there will continue to be times of devoted study, times of worshipful awe, times of pressing ourselves toward obedience and times of sheer, ragged choices to believe, there are new times of just pleasuring in the good company of our Maker.

And so, on that busy morning as lunch awaited, I suddenly saw the idea of a rushed lunch on my feet as ridiculous. Outside my door there was a sunny garden and a quiet front porch. That gently questioning voice told me that this was not the time to push myself through a "working lunch", but rather to pause and enjoy the company of a very dear friend. It wasn't just that I could choose to take time to enjoy a nice lunch in the sunshine. Much deeper than that, I had an opportunity right then to seize the next few moments and enjoy my friendship with God.

Taking a cleansing breath, I slowed my movements and made myself a simple yet nicer meal than I had planned. I walked out to the chairs on my porch and sat down, welcoming God into my break. I smiled at my lunch, smiled at our garden and smiled up at the sky.

Sometimes it's just the smallest pause that helps me remember I have a friend in God.

Responding to God's Friendship

Make a date with God, either right now or in the next few days.
Consider that you will want a distraction-free time, as you choose
your location. Perhaps a shady park or quiet garden would suit
you best.

As you begin… breathe! Take a few minutes to calm yourself, by
excusing distractions from your mind. Center your mind on the
truth that God is present with you and invite Him to make His
presence felt.

Talk to God as if He was visibly present beside you.

Meditate on Jesus' words in John 15:15 for a few minutes:

> *I no longer call you servants, because servants do not
> know their master's business. Instead, I have called
> you friends, for everything that I learned from my
> Father I have made known to you.*

Now, consider some of the following:

How does the thought that God wants to develop a friendship
with you make you *feel*? How would friendship with God change
the way you might approach or relate to God?

How would *enjoying God* affect your life?

Write God a letter, expressing ways in which you would like to
see your relationship with Him grow.

God as Father...

shelter

we will lie down here
pass the night against this rock
that shelters

day ravaged us
whipped us
tore us

but here
the wind
cannot bite through

this crevice
carved to fit us
smells
like
home

God as Father

(Protector–Provider)

I suppose I must have been eighteen. I was puttering around the kitchen, putting this and that away in my mother's neat cupboards. I don't recall very clearly the exact details of the situation, but I remember that I was leaving. I was taking a job some thousand miles away from home for the upcoming summer.

If I could recall the conversation more clearly, I would have a better feel for my father's motivation. Honestly, I just can't bring to mind anything other than one very simple comment he made. Realizing that I would soon be working among people I didn't really know, in an environment that others had found quite stressful, he felt inclined to pass me this little message:

"You don't have to impress anyone, you know. You're just fine the way you are."

No need to impress.

You are just fine.

Close to thirty years later, my father's words still settle and warm me. In what may have seemed to him as an afterthought, my father performed two of the most basic and foundational jobs that a father can perform. With his comment, my father both *protected me* and *provided for me*.

Protection came first in his words. I was immediately protected from the pressure I might have placed on myself to perform for the acceptance of others. Now there is a rightful place for good performance in a job. I'm not belying the responsibility we have to execute the tasks we are given with integrity and to a high standard. But my father was talking about something deeper than job performance.

What my dad was implying was that I was fundamentally OK; a person of character and quality that should be able to face a new situation with confidence and the expectation that I would be a benefit where I was going. My dad was telling me that I could relax into the person that God had already made me to be and expect that my contribution would be a blessing.

Speaking this truth placed a protection around me. It would keep me from the temptation to measure my worth against anyone's expectations. Likewise, it would help me avoid getting into an endless cycle of having to create my own self-worth or sense of self-esteem. His gift of words was disarming, allowing me to step away from the possibility of either of these damaging scenarios.

Provision was also built into my father's words. After protecting me from the losing battle of trying to impress others or live in the fear of their expectations, he provided me with a truth to hold onto: *"You're just fine the way you are."*

Like emergency rations packed into the supplies before a long trek, my father handed me truth that would sustain me when self-worth and self-esteem were flagging.

On their own, my father's words would have been a nice enough blessing, but I'm not sure they would still be protecting and providing for me thirty years later. The reason my father's words still resonate and give me life today is that they reflect the heart of my Father God to me. *His* heart toward me is to protect me and provide for me also, because He is a good Father – the best, in fact.

The notion that God is a good Father is not necessarily easy for people to settle with. Not everyone has experienced things from their human father that reflect God's heart toward us. Even if our human fathers have reflected God's heart at times, there will have been plenty of times when they failed to. That would be the nature of being human.

Yet Scripture calls us to images of God that will redeem our concept of God as Father, if we allow them to. Apparently, God is aware that our experience of human fathers will have been lacking. Maybe this is why He makes such an effort to reveal his Father's heart toward us.

Biblical references to God as a Father are extensive and often cited. Narrowing those down to the example of Christ, we see that Jesus Himself refers to God in this way. In His prayers *to* God, as well as in His conversations *about* God, Jesus calls the Maker of the Universe "Father". Yet Jesus doesn't reserve this title for His own exclusive use. In my conversations with or about my father, I refer to him as "Dad", but I don't expect my friends to do that. I expect them to use his given name. Not so with Jesus. Most famously, when He teaches his disciples how to pray, Jesus begins the prayer, "*Our* Father". *Jesus modeled for us a relationship that knows God as Father.*

But, deeper than simply title, Scripture also reveals God *behaving* as Father. In broader teaching to the crowds that followed Him, Jesus again portrays this Father heart in God. The parable of the prodigal son carries a poignant example. In this story, the father figure is quite obviously the God-figure. This is an important portrayal of Father, because of the huge longing and accepting love the Father shows toward his rebelling son. If there was any sense that God might be a remote, angry or unforgiving Father, this parable uproots that myth to be burned with the other weeds.

The misguided son (who plays our part in the story) is allowed the option to practice his free will and leave home with his inheritance. His father does not control his actions, though these plainly grieve him. During the many months that the son is missing (living fast in an apparent effort to die young), the father aches over him. He longs for him. We know this, because when the son finally does return home, the father sees him way

off down the road. The story says that while the son "was still a long way off" the father saw him. He was scanning the horizon for him! How many times a day he must have stopped his work and looked down the road in hope – in pain – in prayer! The father was longing for this lost boy, scanning the distant horizon for any sign of him.

Next comes the best part: the father *runs* to meet his son. He runs! There is no power play of position here. The father does not require that the son come crawling home, though this is what he fully expected to do. Knowing what he has done, he has probably imagined his father's anger and he only hopes that *maybe* his father will take him back as a servant. The scene has probably played out in his mind – his father contemplating whether or not to even accept him into his presence. This son could never have anticipated that his father would come rushing toward him to throw his arms around him.

And can we imagine that any more, today? Can we imagine that God rushes toward us with arms open, as we turn our steps toward him?

It's not only the New Testament images of God that reveal a father. The Old Testament is filled with fatherly imagery too; but I will only cite one. Psalm 91 is the quintessential psalm of protection and provision, those fatherly qualities that we have already mentioned. Looking at the first few verses, consider what they are telling us:

Whoever who dwells in the shelter of the Most High
will rest in the shadow of the Almighty.
I will say of the Lord,
"He is my refuge and my fortress,
my God, in whom I trust."
Surely he will save you from the fowler's snare
and from the deadly pestilence.
He will cover you with his feathers
and under his wings you will find refuge;
his faithfulness will be your shield and rampart.

The poet's images are clear. He's speaking of protection when he uses words like *shelter, shadow* and *fortress.* This God will *save you* and *cover you.* He will *provide* for you *a shield* and *a rampart,* or fortification.

The image of God as a protecting Father is very important, because so many people today have felt anything but protected in life. Even a father with the best intentions can't possibly keep his children sheltered from every hurt. It's physically, mathematically and every other way impossible.

One of my earliest memories from childhood is of a painful encounter with other children. I was four years old, and my family had recently moved from the United States to Sweden. I remember that we lived in an apartment that was three or four flights up. I suppose my older siblings must have ventured down the stairs with me, but my memory is of a terrible feeling of loneliness and grief as neighborhood children laughed at me in the playground. I couldn't speak the language yet, and the little mob of locals taunted me for my inability to communicate.

"How could anyone be so stupid as to not know the language all around them?" they must have thought. The conclusions that children draw are cruel and the pleasure they take in belittling those who are different is legendary.

My point is the significance that one of my clearest early childhood memories is of pain. And painful things will always happen. My human father failed to protect me from every single hurt in life precisely because it would have been impossible for him to do so. Still, God used him to reflect God's heart of protection to me.

Scripture refers to God as "Father", shows Him behaving as a Father and then records His mandate to us to also behave in fatherly ways. God's instructions to His people reveal what is important to Him and what is on His heart. And His desires regarding the powerless and the fatherless are clear. God asks us to care for them; to live His Father love toward them. Proverbs instructs us not to take advantage of the fatherless regarding their fields and crops. Old Testament law requires that aliens, orphans and widows be properly looked out for. There is a strong sense of fatherhood in Psalm 68:6 where it speaks of God setting "the lonely in families". God is filling in the gaps for us, asking us to care for each other; making sure that those without family are folded in.

The blessing of living with God as this protective, provision-making father is that there are great promises inherent in this relationship. Psalm 91 tells us we *will not fear* the many horrible things listed: that is, a lot of *really bad stuff* that could happen to us in life. But let's get out of biblical language and think about what the "snares, arrows, plagues and pestilence" of this psalm might be in our lives today.

For me, I live in a place where violent robbery is an issue. Because of how things are done in many parts of Africa, personal security is exactly that – a personal issue. The city or sovereign state is not set up to attend to the individual security of each citizen, the way it would be in most western countries, where taxpayers can expect a certain level of active protection day in and day out. All of this is to say that my family's and my own situation requires that we attend to security issues ourselves. We hire a security company that will send a team of tough guys in a truck, should we hit the alarm button. We have a night watchman, who spends the long hours of darkness alert in our garden. And, while I would rather my windows displayed only the splendid African sky, we must also have bars on every window and bolted gates across our doors at night. These are the prudent ways that we live in the reality of our situation.

But do we fear? I suppose there might be times when a spike of fear pops up in our minds, as it might in any city, but I can honestly say that we do not live with the constant drain of a present fear. Psalm 91's promise is real to us. We will not fear the "terror of night". In fact, we take it one step further as we appropriate the promise of Psalm 4:8. We will "lie down and sleep in peace, for you alone, O Lord, make [us] dwell in safety" (NIV).

Psalm 91 goes on to say that our Father God protects us and we won't fear plague and pestilence. Today's plagues and pestilences are aggressive and borderless. There is the plague of cancer and other diseases (old and new, ever morphing and confounding us) that have grown to epidemic proportions around the world. Don't forget depression and suicide, on the rise in unprecedented numbers in societies the world over. There is the pestilence of toxins so innumerable that ridding our homes of all of them has become pretty much an impossible task. Again, we do what we can to be responsible in these areas, but we don't live in fear. We have a protective Father who has promised to be a shelter around us.

As only a father can, God also speaks directly to us about

fear. He says, "Don't do it. Do *not* fear." Throughout Scripture, God's voice comes through clearly, commanding that we do not fear. While there are many things that the Bible seems to say we might have to live with, from suffering to misunderstanding to hunger or poverty, fear is never listed as something we should learn to accept. Instead, we are always told plainly to reject it.

When my children were small and had a bad dream, or experienced some of the natural fear of the dark, I always told them not to be afraid. My husband and I never told the kids to just accept the fear and go to sleep. Not a chance! We told them not to fear because we were there. We might be down the hall from them, but they were not alone.

And this is exactly God's promise to us. We don't need to fear, because He is with us. Joshua 1:9 is just one of the many places that says it boldly:

> *Be strong and courageous. Do not be terrified; do not be discouraged, for the Lord your God will be with you wherever you go.*

And this is where the psalmist goes as he brings Psalm 91 to a close: *God is with us.* First and foremost, the psalm assures us that we have a Father God who is actively protecting us and providing for us. This is the strong ground we stand on. And yet the psalm doesn't say that we will never encounter danger, pain, suffering or hardship. Instead, right in the midst of the attack, we can expect God to be with us because that is His promise to us. The Psalm goes on…

> *"Because they love me," says the Lord, "I will rescue them;*
> *I will protect them, for they acknowledge my name;*
> *They will call upon me, and I will answer them;*
> *I will be with them in trouble,*
> *I will deliver them and honor them."*

Stubborn in His Father love for us, He sticks right with us in every situation, soothing and encouraging us with His presence. But there is a requirement for us. Psalm 91 suggests that these promises are true for those who *have made God* their dwelling place.

> *Whoever dwells in the shelter of the Most High*
> *will rest in the shadow of the Almighty.*

Later, it says (91:9–10),

> *If you say "The Lord is my refuge,"*
> *and you make the Most High your dwelling,*
> *no harm will overtake you,*
> *no disaster will come near your tent.*

There is action required on our part. We choose to make Him our shelter and to come under His care. We make Him our dwelling. But what does that mean? How do we experience God as our shelter and dwelling place in the same way that the psalmist has mentioned in the ninetieth poem?

As if building toward a theme, Psalm 90 confirms God as our shelter, prior to the promises of Psalm 91:

> *Lord, you have been our dwelling place*
> *throughout all generations.*

I believe that making God my dwelling is to base myself in Him. Just as my home is my shelter, where I rest and retreat, God is my home – the place where my heart rests, shelters and is refreshed. He is the foundation I stand on, the refuge I settle in.

When Santa Barbara's terrible Tea Fire swept through the campus where my sons were studying in 2008, the college sent updates saying the students would "shelter in place" in the designated safe location of the concrete gymnasium. This gym was the predetermined refuge for the college and her nearest neighbors. As the fire approached, the community retreated into its strong shelter.

Likewise, we can shelter in the safe place provided for us under the protective care of Father God. To make Him my dwelling is to have predetermined that He is my safest base, my one true home. It requires that I acknowledge that He is the best place for me and that I say yes to the protection that He is offering through relationship with Him. Unlike any other form of protection offered to us, this is the huge love and acceptance of the Prodigal's father that simultaneously brings protection as we embrace it. But it's a choice we make.

As we choose to accept this love, we nestle into Him and base our lives in the shelter of our relationship with Him. Living in the shelter doesn't mean I have been pulled out of normal life and no longer relate to the world around me. Instead, it means that my foundation is firmly rooted in His love.

For me, these times of nestling often come early in the morning as I am waking. There are mornings when I just feel God's presence hovering close as my mind comes to consciousness. There is palpable sheltering warmth very near, and I find myself comfortably at home within it. On the days when this safe place under His wings is the most keenly felt, I often just linger there. I say "Yes" to dwelling in the shelter of the Most High and I allow myself the pleasure of just feeling and enjoying it for a while.

The prodigal son had an action required of him, as well. He needed *to go home*. His father rushed toward him as he came home, but it was the son who had made that initial choice to return. It's important to note that the father didn't wait to accept him until he was all the

way home. Instead, he met him on the road. Being on the road suggests movement and process and the idea that the mess of his son's life is not quite all sorted out yet. He goes out and meets him there, on the way, destination still unreached. And God meets us in our incomplete process, as well. He meets us as soon as we turn toward Him, in the middle of our mess. He doesn't hold back until we have cleaned ourselves up and reached some level of perfection. Father God runs to embrace us as we move toward Him. But the turn in His direction is ours to make.

Living in this protected place, where I am provided for, accepted and freely loved, I am able to experience God as the Father He longs to be to me. As His created child, I have no need to struggle with the insecurity that comes from trying to impress those around me. My human father's voice comes back to me across many years, and I rest in the truth he conveyed from Father God. In the deepest, widest, truest, most all-encompassing meaning of the words, I am loved by a really good Dad.

Responding to God as Father

Make a date with God, either right now or in the next few days. Clear enough space in your schedule so as not to rush through this time.

As you begin, imagine that you are entering a sheltered place of protection. Enter God's presence as you would enter a favorite safe and peaceful spot.

Turn your mind toward God as a good Father. Take a few minutes to allow yourself into the sense of being His son or daughter.

If the father image immediately stops you cold, ask God to help you see what it is that stops you from being able to embrace him as Father. Is there a hurt or disappointment that damages your image of Him as a good Father?

Take a few minutes to read the story of the Prodigal in Luke 15:11–32. Try to feel some of the emotions that the wandering son felt as he began to realize his mistake. What does he feel as he envisions his father? Try to feel some of the emotions that the father experienced as he had no contact with his lost son. What did he feel as the days without him continued to add up? Think through their reunion and what each of them felt.

Consider the following:

Can you recall a time you felt God's extravagant love toward you?

What has His all-encompassing acceptance of you looked or felt like in your life?

When and how have you felt God's protection in the past?

When and how have you experienced His provision for you?

In what areas of your life do you feel you need a good father today?

Write a letter to God, addressing him as "Dad", and talk to Him about those needs now.

God as Mother...

source

not from the pungent earth
though her dark loam
hosts a thousand rich reasons to live
no, not from her round form
do i come

not from the pale leaves
the slender grasses on the plains
though they present fine feasting
no, not from this foliage
do i feed

not from the clear spring
sweeter than summer's first shy wine
lighter even than new rain
no, not from this dimpling pool
do i drink

these tender things
they feed me
it's true
and of the malleable clay, yes,
you formed me

but i come from your heart
from under your breast hidden

and on your lap
you nourished me
encircled me
sustained me
emboldened me

mother God
i long for you
still

God as Mother

(Nurturer–Life-giver)

The knot in my shoulder had progressed from being merely annoying to actually causing a headache. I tried to look unaffected, but the awkward motion of my neck as I went about my day was apparent.

"What's up?" Byron asked.

"Oh, my neck is stiff," I said. "Kind of knotted up."

"But how did it get knotted up?" he asked.

"Well, I was holding the baby," I replied, as if that should make it all perfectly clear.

His eyes widened a little, with the wordless question "And?"

"I was holding the baby for kind of a long time, while he slept, and I had my head in sort of a weird position in order to keep him comfortable, so he would stay asleep."

We were traveling a lot in those days. We were in and out of people's homes visiting friends and family, before we returned to East Africa. There wasn't a lot of routine. Some days I was listening to a lecture on how to effectively learn a new language, our little son in tow. Other days I was careening through the shops filling my cart with what I thought were the essentials for the next few years stretching ahead of us in remote places. Again, our little son was always in tow.

With life a bit on the road and suitcases as our normal entourage, calm rhythms of daily life evaporated and a well-napped baby was hard to come by. I just remember that, on this day, the nap had been in my arms and I didn't want to bring it to an end until it had had sufficient time to do its good work.

Looking no less puzzled – in fact maybe a little more so – Byron sighed.

"Wow," he said. "I would never let my neck knot up just so the baby could sleep."

It wasn't a particularly admiring *or* a particularly critical response. It was just a fact as he saw it. But it made me smile.

"And that," I said, a wee bit cheekily, "is why *you* are not the mommy."

A mom heart and a dad heart – this baby of ours was in need of both.

And so are we. We need to know both the fatherly heart of God and the motherly one.

Now, I'm not suggesting that God actually has two hearts. What I'm suggesting is that God's heart is big enough to encompass all that is traditionally thought of as male characteristics as well as all that may have traditionally been thought of as female characteristics. Our ability to appreciate this fullness of God is curtailed when we are limited to seeing God through the lens of male-only imagery. When it says in Genesis

(1:27) that God created "human beings in his… image… male and female he created them", it means that his image carries within it all the qualities that both genders reflect. To degenerate into an argument about whether God is male or female is not actually helpful at this point. I'm not trying to assign gender. God is something beyond our understanding, and whether or not God has a gender, or what that gender is, is not the point of my ponderings. The purpose of pursuing the female imagery of God is not to reduce God to anything, but to allow God's fullness to appear more clearly to us.

Some of the most beautiful images of God in Scripture are feminine and decidedly motherly. In Matthew 23:37 Jesus uses the picture of a mother hen, collecting her chicks under her wings, as He describes how He longs to care for Jerusalem. Unless you've seen this happen, you can't appreciate how fantastic it is. When a bird of prey would pass even very high above our garden in Africa, our fluffy mama hens would transform from docile farmyard inhabitants to vigilant living fortresses in a turbo-second. There was a mom-call that they employed at these moments, and the chicks dove directly under their wings to be hidden totally as soon as they heard it. The image of a chicken might not strike you as beautiful; but getting beyond poultry and thinking of the way the mother hen uses her own body to hide her chicks brings a moving image of selfless love that is lovely indeed.

In Hosea 11:4, God speaks to the children of Israel and says that He is the one who taught them to walk; He took them by the arms to lead them. It goes on:

> *I led them with cords of human kindness,*
> *with ties of love.*
> *To them I was like one who lifts*
> *a little child to the cheek,*
> *and I bent down to feed them.*

These are very motherly images of tender care for a small child. I'm not suggesting that they are one hundred per cent exclusively motherly, any more than I would suggest that the images of protection and provision we looked at in "God as Father" are totally and exclusively fatherly. Those things are *predominantly* fatherly, just as these images of teaching a child to walk are *predominantly* motherly. As we allow ourselves to think of God in a motherly way, we will find ourselves able to experience a deeper understanding of the nature of God's love for us.

I say all this because there seems to be a fear or resistance in some spheres of Christianity that would keep people from being able to experience this aspect of God. Maybe it's a fear of goddess worship, or perhaps a fear of Jesus' mother being almost deified by some. But recognizing motherly characteristics in God is not the same as creating a goddess, calling God female or worshipping Mary. A dear friend of mine here in Africa is a former

Catholic priest. He and I were chatting one afternoon about how the motherly characteristics of God can be so comforting and so helpful, especially in certain situations.

"Alfonse," I said to him as we looked out into the garden, "do you think that so many people have such a strong hunger for Mary to be more than human because we've failed to highlight the softer, more motherly things of God in the spectrum of characteristics that are present in God?"

"Yes," he said quietly. "I really think that could be it. We've left some parts missing."

But I don't want to leave some of the characteristics of God missing. I want the full array of characteristics that both male and female images of God reveal, so that my heart might learn to know this God in the beauty and richness that Scripture portrays.

God was dreaming of me as I was being formed. Even before I was formed, I was thought of. God was dreaming of me, just as a mother dreams of the one she carries within her. It's not particularly common for a father to lie awake at night dreaming of the child, smaller than a kidney bean, growing quietly inside his wife. On the other hand, it is entirely common that the mother is doing this. By sheer virtue of the fact that she can feel the changes in her physical being, be they ever so slight, a newly pregnant mother's mind immediately begins to engage with this child. It's the start of their relationship, this pondering.

She is physically, emotionally and spiritually aware of the child's presence. And, more so than is common to a man, a mother will have imagined a child even before her child is conceived or born.

It is tremendously comforting to realize that God is aware of me in the same way. In the first chapter of Jeremiah (verse 5) God declares, "Before I formed you in the womb I knew you, before you were born I set you apart." Thoughts of who I am, who my *true person* is, were in God's mind before I was even conceived. God was dreaming of me.

Scripture tells us that God knows the days of my life, my coming and going, the hairs on my head. He is aware of my rising and my settling down. God declares that I am His workmanship, created for good works in Christ that have been prepared *beforehand* for me to walk in. There is no mass design for humanity. Instead, Scripture is clear that each of us is individually designed and given characteristics and gifts that make us uniquely who we are. We have a unique set of gifts and strengths and personality traits with which to reflect God's love to the world.

Again, this intimate thought toward each child is a motherly quality in God. It's not that a father could not or would not think of his young, developing child. Rather, it is predominantly common to mothers to be tuned in to the person who is not yet here. While a human mother does not have the power that God does to design who this child will be, she does have that heart that is dreaming over this little one.

Even after birth, in the early years of development, this is frequently the primary engagement of the mother. As the Magi came to Bethlehem and presented their gifts, Mary mulled over all the amazing events that had surrounded the arrival of her baby. The Scripture says Mary held all these things in her heart, and I believe that this is because Mary was the mother. Joseph was no less of a good parent for not pondering all these things. The minute the angel appeared and told him to move to Egypt in order to protect the child, he did it. He didn't hesitate to carry out his fatherly duties. But Mary was *musing over* all these things. Mary was holding this child, and all that was surrounding His life, in her heart.

Having dreamt of us, God, like our human mother, is our life-giver as well: the one from whom we draw existence. In a perfect reflection of the fullness of God, it takes both man and woman to create a child. But once that child has been created in the hidden folds of a woman's body, she is the source of life and nurture during the all-critical months of gestation. The umbilical cord itself is a testimony to this, as all sustenance is first processed and then passed on to the baby directly from the mother. It's a beautiful symbol of our utter dependence on God as we are shaped into who we are.

Like all of Creation, a mother's body can teach us about

the One who designed it. A woman's body is made to provide for her unborn child, and she craves an increase in nutritious foods as the body of her child is being built. If she doesn't take in enough healthy calories during pregnancy, the baby will not develop well. But the female body is so committed to the healthy development of her child that it will fight to grow a strong baby, even if a mother will not or cannot take in what is required to do so. In an all-out effort to make sure that this child has what she needs, a mother's body will rob from itself before allowing the developing baby to go without. Her bones and teeth and hair will suffer as minerals are stripped from her to build her child. Her muscles will be mined for protein. Her body senses the needs of the child and sacrifices itself for that child.

This physical reality of how a woman's body is designed reflects God's heart toward us, for this is the kind of God we have. We have a God who made a sacrifice in order to make sure we have life. We have a God who gave Christ's living body to provide for us what we needed to become truly alive.

The poet David refers to a motherly image as he explains himself to God in Psalm 131 (TNIV):

My heart is not proud, Lord,
my eyes are not haughty;
I do not concern myself with great matters
or things too wonderful for me.

But I have calmed myself
and quieted my ambitions.
I am like a weaned child with its mother;
like a weaned child I am content.
Israel, put your hope in the Lord
both now and for evermore.

Other translations say the weaned child "rests against its mother"
or "sits in its mother's lap". David is saying, "I'm able to sit here
with you like a weaned child with his mother. I am quietly calm,
here in your lap." History suggests that the normal age of weaning
in these ancient times would have been at about the age of three.
Even today, women in many cultures continue the breastfeeding
bond until a child is two or three years old.

Bearing this in mind, this is how I hear this psalm…

My heart is not proud and conceited, dear Lord,
my eyes are not looking arrogantly around.
I am not caught up in things that I can't possibly
understand; not bogged down by matters that are
way beyond me. Instead, I have calmed my mind and
quieted my soul. Like a weaned child sitting calmly
with her mother, I sit here with you.
O Israel, O all nations who are in turmoil,
put your hope in this good God, now and for ever.

As a mother who joyfully participated in the natural process of breastfeeding my babies, I have a real sense for why the child in the psalm sits calmly and quietly with the mother. The weaned child is deeply secure, having experienced possibly years of nurture in her mother's lap. For two or three years there was warmth, safety, nurture, comfort, provision and nutrition present in this very lap. Now, as natural development has progressed and the need for actual nutritional provision from the mother's body has ended, this child still feels the blessing of the years of bonding. This child *knows* what closeness and nurture feel like, and just leaning against the mother brings that all back. There is an established bond that is calming to the young child, and this is the foundation that the child lives from.

Thus, as life carries on and things become less simple, the poet still remembers that God has cared for his every need. He can rest next to God, leaning quietly beside this One who has given life and nurture for so many years. In this place right next to God, the poet king does not have to understand everything. Here he can rest, knowing that someone else has a handle on it.

I have no idea how many thousands of air miles I have traveled with a toddler on my lap. Having raised four children in a highly mobile international family means that I have crisscrossed the globe many times over with a child buckled against me. In all those years of holding little ones on airplanes, the children never had to do anything other than stay resting on my lap. Where we were going, how the plane worked and when we would arrive were, by and large, things beyond their understanding. Their only job was to settle into my lap.

I want to learn to live more easily from God's lap in this way. Lately, as I've meditated on this psalm more and more, it seems that I've been given many opportunities to practice climbing into this place. Seemingly impossible situations present themselves and I find myself overwhelmed by anxiety in my need to fix the mess I see around me. In these situations I find it really challenging to retain any semblance of the calm of the weaned child in the psalm. Yet I long to learn to depend on God and to see those details that are so far out of my control taken care of.

Still, my tendency – in fact my strong inclination – is to jump down from God's lap and run screaming in circles instead.

On a recent trip to a far-away community, something went wrong with our car. Halfway into the bone-jarring twelve-hour journey there, the battery pooped out, and we were left to push-start it any time we needed it to move. After five days of this, the electrics were randomly cutting out and killing the engine as we drove along. We could push it back to life again... *most* of the time. It honestly didn't help that all three of the adult males on the trip were strongly mechanically minded. The fact that the symptoms were stumping even them only increased my anxiety over the situation.

I could feel my panic rising. We had guests with us on this week-long trip, guests who needed to make it back to town to meet non-refundable flights. We could *not* get stuck hundreds of miles from anywhere in "the bush". We could not simply end up marooned in some distant hills while my father and our friends all missed their flights. I could feel myself wanting to hyperventilate. I could feel my stomach nervously waiting to go into convulsions as I considered the reality of the miles between us and help.

This particular set of circumstances played perfectly into my set of issues. For whatever reason, I have a really tense response to travel problems and I carry a false sense of responsibility to get everyone through their journeys safely and on time. I'm sure it has to do with the many, many flights we've made with slim connections and complicated itineraries. My anxiety increases dramatically when it's my kids who are crossing the world and I'm aware of the impossibly few minutes between their flights. It's something I had wanted to learn to handle better… and God seemed to agree on that need.

"Lap of God!" I kept thinking. "I must sit in the lap of God and quiet my panicked mind." I had *no* power to make the engine run or guarantee our timely return to town. I had to stop fretting over matters outside my control. It may sound small, but at the time the issue was blowing up into a major catastrophe in my mind. And it was just one in a series of out-of-control travel scenarios that I had been experiencing. Clearly, God was trying to help me confront my tendency to worry and learn to trust Him. Over and over, I envisioned the peaceful lap I was invited to sit in. Over and over, I practiced sitting there, giving over the things that I could not control.

With many more push-starts and a few mysterious engine cut-outs, just for good measure, we did finally make it back to "civilization" in time to get everyone easily to their flights. And I'm pretty sure that the lessons learned were specifically for me.

As I learn to trust in the midst of these "small" disasters, my faith expands and I grow to be more like the child in the psalm, who is able to rest in the presence of her mother, not worried about the things that are too great for her. My little traumas when the car threatens to keep us from getting our visitors to their connections serve as training exercises that help me in the face of the real traumas that are seriously too great for me. Because I have experienced the close care of this God who is looking over the details with intimate attention, I am emboldened to trust for much graver matters.

This process of experiencing God's faithfulness and recalling it is how the Children of Israel learned as well. The Psalms include portions of reflection that recount the history of God's faithfulness in very specific ways. One of the most beautiful spiritual practices that we see in the Old Testament is this call to remember the stories of God's past care. I love the image of the gathered community, recounting the many ways God has been faithful to them as a nation.

Lamentations 3:21–22 tells us why remembering is so good for us:

> *Yet this I call to mind*
> *and therefore I have hope:*
> *Because of the Lord's great love we are not consumed,*
> *for his compassions never fail.*

As the children of God look back on the history of God's unfailing compassion, hope rises in their hearts. And this is the lesson of the weaned child. The weaned child remembers that her every past need has been faithfully met by the mother that she now rests against. She rests there still, holding the clear memories that teach her that this is where she can release things that are too great for her and choose to simply trust.

I long to be more like the weaned child, embracing the motherly qualities of God and leaning quietly against the one who has faithfully cared for me, even dreaming of me long before I was born. Surely this is where hope for the days ahead is built, on the solid foundation of the history of days past.

Responding to God as Mother

Make a date with God, either right now or in the next few days.

As you come into God's presence, let go of tensions and think about what it might feel like to lean quietly against God. Allow yourself to simply rest there for a few moments.

Meditate on the image from Hosea 11:3–4 of God teaching you to walk. Envision God as a mother, bending down to take your arms and lead you as you attempt your first steps. Think about the smile on a mother's face as she encourages her little one forward, praising every clumsy step.

These verses say that God bent down to feed the children of Israel. Allow yourself to think about the God of all Creation stooping down to your level to meet your needs. What does this picture of God teach you about God's feelings for you?

God told Jeremiah that he was known before he was formed and consecrated him before he was born. God was dreaming of Jeremiah and God dreamt of each one of us as well. If you were to guess what God was dreaming over your life, what would you say it was?

Remembering God's faithfulness to us in the past gives us hope for the future. Take some time to recall ways in which God has cared for you in the past year, or even longer. If you have time, look back across many years and remember God's faithfulness.

The child in Psalm 131 is not stressing about things too great for his or her understanding. What are some things that weigh on you that you could release to God's faithfulness? Allow the history of faithfulness to give you hope as you look into the months ahead.

Spend a little time journaling about what motherly images of God teach you, and how you feel when you think of God in the feminine. Talk to God about specific areas in your life that could use a mother's touch right now.

God as Artist...

breathing to know you

God, i breathe you in
the sweet-strong
full-ripe lingering

i see you
in warm colors
across the sky

i see you
dance broad leaves
in the wind

i see you
like a thousand lit lilies
burning on the waves

i sit here quietly
breathing
to know you

God as Artist

(Creativity)

I stepped into the prayer room and was immediately enveloped in a warm, almost fragrant presence. Paint drips and finger smudges, candle stubs, Post-it notes, wide canvases of butcher paper, soft lumps of clay, crayons, markers, pastels, fabrics, pebbles, ashes; the room was cluttered beautifully with the supplies, the product and the cast-offs of artists. Great swaths of color made bold prayers. Scribblings of poetry revealed hearts. Passionate letters of longing or declaration, of shy hopes and big dreams hung unashamedly upon the transformed walls.

Forty-eight hours earlier, this had been just a normal room. It was a fairly boring office space, void of creative energy, purely functional, with its simple desk, shelves and rudimentary supplies. But all of that was gone now. With expectation and some muscle power, we hauled the office furnishings out and, with them, the sense of regiment and routine. The room then stood starkly bare and somewhat cold, but, with a little imagination, the possibilities for transformation were endless.

We wanted to meet with God. As a group of friends, we wanted to clear some space in our hearts and heads, in our building and in our schedules to allow for God's invasion into our lives. Inspired by stories from others around the world, we called this week a Prayer Week and this space a Prayer Room. Dividing the seven days into 168 hourly slots, we made a spreadsheet of sorts. We passed the spreadsheet amongst friends, inviting people to sign up for time with God in the prayer space that we were designing to fill the emptied office.

The naked office began to morph into something beautiful. We covered the windows with fabulous fabrics, draped little lights across the wrought-iron curtain rods and filled the newly claimed area with simple supplies. Every inch of wall was covered in broad sheets of paper. Painting, drawing and sketching supplies were laid out in abundance. We set candles on little tables covered in richly colored cloth, choosing warm fragrances like vanilla to sweeten the air. A modest music system was installed, with a broad variety of CDs that would encourage prayer yet fit any mood. There was a pillowed corner to rest in, an iron kettle with scraps of paper and a box of matches where we could burn our confessions and leave regrets behind. We set a table with bread and wine, designated a wailing wall where we could post prayer requests for others to join us in and, most importantly, told everyone who entered that this was a free space to be with God. This was a rule-free environment, where coming into God's presence could be experienced in whatever way you felt you needed that to be.

Now, with only forty-eight hours of occupancy, the room was already an explosion of color and written words. Paintings prayed from the walls. Words cried out from emboldened hearts. Poetry asked for healing. Sculptures declared freedom. And this was just the beginning. Twice in the week we would replace half the wallpaper to give more room for expression.

Our community of friends learned a lot from that first week of dedicated prayer space. Perhaps the thing that stood out to me the most was the simple revelation that God's presence releases creative energy and expression in people. These were the same people whom I had prayed with on numerous other occasions throughout the years. We had sat quietly with eyes closed and murmured our words of supplication many times.

Was there something wrong with the conventional idea of prayer? No, there really wasn't. If there was anything wrong with it, it was only that it was limited. Perhaps better said, it was *limiting*. The biggest lesson we learned from that week was that when people approach God outside of the box of their perception of prayer – when they are encouraged to express themselves to him in any way that they might choose – the results can come flooding out in the form of art.

OK, so not all the art was showroom quality. Most of the poems and paintings were not actually crying out with their perfection to be seen by the world. But these heart-prayers were creative expression and pieces of art nonetheless. And this should come as no surprise, for God is, after all, an artist. In fact, God is The Artist.

God is a creative God. (And I think that might be the world's greatest understatement!) God is a creative God. Say it slowly. Punctuate each syllable. This is truth.

The obvious first revelation of this is the creation account in Genesis. The story portrays an artist-God who loves His work. It starts with a vision in the heart and mind of God. His idea is percolating now and He's seeing our universe, with us in the thick of it. Oh, this idea is too beautiful to rush! It is too detailed to *blink* into existence. The Spirit of God is brooding over this development and beginning to breathe it out. He can see even the tiniest details in His mind. And now He begins to speak it into existence.

As God expresses His vision, He reveals His endless capacities as an artist. It's pouring out of Him like clear water from a spring. He is imagining little beetles and giant whales. He is picturing golden grasses moving softly in the evening breeze. He is thinking of thunderstorms and snowfall. He is envisioning fire-colored leaves and plump, glowing fruit. He is holding mountain ranges, yet designing butterflies. He's brushing trees with ten thousand shades of green, washing oceans with a million hues of blue.

God could have made this whole thing with so much less attention to detail. He could have designed our world without such extravagant flair. Leaves could easily fall to the ground without the jaw-dropping colors. The sun could rise and set without a full-on riot of palette and light. A thousand kinds of flowers would have been enough. Aren't innumerable kinds a bit over the top? And people: why make each one unique? Why allow endless combinations of personalities and giftings to complicate and enrich every human interaction and endeavor? Four basic types could have possibly been adequate, don't you think?

But what does all this creativity flowing in the heart of God have to do with us? What does any of this mean to us as we approach Him?

My first thought is that God is desperate to show Himself to us. He is literally pulling out every stop to communicate and draw our attention to who He is. God wants us to notice Him!

In Psalm 19 the poet king recognizes this. The first four verses say:

> *The heavens declare the glory of God;*
> *the skies proclaim the work of his hands.*
> *Day after day they pour forth speech;*
> *night after night they display knowledge.*
> *They have no speech, they use no words;*
> *no sound is heard from them.*
> *Yet their voice goes out into all the earth,*
> *their words to the ends of the world.*

What is David telling us here? The open skies are talking about

God! The endless depth of blue, the gauze-like traces of cloud and those that are ponderously huge and heavy with rain, they are speaking to us. The Northern Lights and the Southern Cross are drawing our breath, because they are whispering truth. There is no place on earth where their voices are not heard. They speak every language.

You see, God is very well acquainted with the limitations of our minds. We are a fallible and forgetful bunch. We don't remember that God made this beautiful earth and placed us on it. Instead, we argue over how He made it, some demanding to know *if* He made it at all, and what His intentions are for our place in it. Collectively, we move away from the knowledge we have of Him and move toward our own ideas. So God has surrounded us with displays of His handiwork that point us – if we are looking – to Him.

The idea that Creation is to be valued is something that most people understand today. It's as if we are all coming out of a machine age and lifting our eyes higher to the hills, the trees, the mountains and the skies and saying to each other, "Wow! We were forgetting these things! Look! Enjoy! Value! Protect!" My encouragement here to those whose eyes are feasting on this world around them is, "Don't stop with what you see!" We need to lift our chins a little higher and see that, beyond Creation, there is a Creator; a Creator who wants to be recognized.

The controversy seems to have been that people either

focus on the Creation or the Creator. But should we separate art and artist in this way? Would we look at Van Gogh's *Starry Night* and say, "This is so beautiful! This is so precious! This is so worth saving! This should be protected! This needs to be cherished and passed on intact for our children and grandchildren! But Van Gogh... well, we don't really believe there was such an artist. But this piece of art! Wow!"

Likewise, we would not honor Van Gogh without recognizing the brilliance and value of his work. We would not praise the man and his gifting yet disregard, diminish or destroy his paintings. Instead, we build a museum to protect, preserve and display what he created.

We understand the link between art and artist in our physical world. Let's not forget it in the bigger, beyond-our-understanding world. Creation speaks to us of the Artist who created her. We need to listen. God is an Artist who has extravagantly set His work all around us that we might notice Him. Indeed, God is an Artist who wants to be discovered.

Once we recognize that God is revealing Himself through His Creation, He can use His art to communicate with us. He can pass us messages, if you like, and relay truth through His displayed work.

I live in Africa, where much of Creation still reflects its original state. I have the enormous privilege of walking in places that really have not seen much significant development at all.

My family has followed shallow streams through quiet twists and turns, coming upon zebra and gazelle that perk their ears toward us in surprise as they consider their escape routes. We have camped under starry skies with only the warm wind as a canopy over us. We have bathed in clear pools fed by warm springs.

Here, in these magnificent places, God speaks to us. When we lived 100 miles from a paved road and four hours of hard driving from a telephone or a post office, our house sat on the side of a hill that sloped down gently to a chattering stream. The beauty of our remote location was such that if I tried to describe it to you, you would think I was making it up.

But that beauty became more to us than a pleasant backdrop to life. Because God spoke through it, the beauty sustained us. As much as we loved our work, and as much as we respected and admired our neighbors, living as the only western family in a remote place wasn't always easy. Trying to bring appropriate and sensitive community development to a people who were at times receptive, at times aggressively unreceptive, at times welcoming and at times quite hostile, meant that the ten years in that community carried pain and joy in equal measure. When a neighbor employed our simple suggestions to terrace his fields and feed his gardens with natural mulch and fertilizer, it was a great joy to see the abundant harvest from his land. Yet when still another friend's baby died of simple dehydration from diarrhea caused by lack of clean water and sterile baby bottles, it hurt deeply. Boiling the water first and keeping bottles clean is a simple lesson, but my teaching it didn't make anyone practice it.

In these times of discouragement and struggle, the very hills were a comfort to us. Standing at the window in our bedroom, I would take the view of the rolling, grassy hills into my body like sustenance. But lest we be confused about the source of that sustenance, it wasn't the hills that were feeding me.

Again, David knows this full well. Consider the first two verses of Psalm 121 (NIV):

> *I lift up my eyes to the hills –*
> *where does my help come from?*
> *My help comes from the Lord,*
> *the Maker of heaven and earth.*

The psalm goes on with promises of the Lord's care over us as we go about this business of life, but these first two verses make a strong point. "Where does my help come from? My help comes from the Lord." And how do I know this? I lifted my eyes to the hills and the hills reminded me of this truth.

Creation speaks of her Creator. In this case, the steadfastness of the hills, never leaving, always shining there in the afternoon sun – ancient, lovely, welcoming – these hills told me that God was there. He didn't disappear and leave me in hard times. He was solid, steadfast, lasting. I lifted my eyes, saw His handiwork, and remembered Him.

But is the only purpose of God's art to point us to Him? I believe that God's art is also for our enjoyment, because God values art, beauty and the aesthetically pleasing. God likes things to look good. In fact, God is so into beauty that He didn't stop at the creation of an abundantly beautiful world. When the time came for the Children of Israel to create their first holy place, the Tabernacle, God had very specific ideas that He passed on to them about how to decorate it. Exodus 31:6 says that not only did God design intricate details to adorn the place of His presence, but He placed skill in the artisans so that they would be able to create what He had asked them to. This confirms again to me that God is a creative God who is seriously into art. God appreciates a beautiful setting, be it natural or man-made, and He is willing to touch individuals in order to create it.

God designed us to appreciate and benefit from beauty and art. It is pleasant to be surrounded by loveliness. There is inherent value in the well-being that the natural environment and man-made beauty produce in us. Beauty and art feel good. Sitting in a quiet park in the shade of the trees calms and refreshes us. It might even inspire us.

When the New Testament says that Jesus came to give us life and life to the full, I believe it means just that: *to the full.* That's what it says. Life is not full if it is lived only on one plane. We might be spiritually in touch with our Maker and yet totally off kilter in the wholeness of life. We were made to enjoy beauty, nature, and the artistic gifts of others. We are not only spiritual beings but also sensual beings who are made to find pleasure in good things. When we see God as an Artist who values all these forms of beauty, we are released to value them ourselves.

The freedom to enjoy and value art and beauty can be stifled by many different things. In Africa, where life is so difficult for so many of the population, the hard work of daily life can reduce people to a focus on hand-to-mouth survival. The people who are literally struggling from one meal to the next are not always inclined to cherish the artistic. Life is simply too hard and that value has often been crushed in them.

In the West, where life can be one long rush toward material gain, art is often appreciated, but frequently for the wrong reasons. The cash value of a piece of work is, at times, what causes a Western person to enjoy a piece of art. In the West, there is a need to return to the simple appreciation of the way a branch moves in the wind. Wherever we find ourselves in the world, we need the Creative Spirit of God to renew our appreciation of these things.

In my line of work, I can easily be overwhelmed by despair. Living and working in Africa can easily dishearten me, when the statistics alone threaten to stop me dead in my tracks. The number of child soldiers; the number of deaths due to preventable disease; the number of people without clean water or a viable income… it's all too much for the mind to hold. My heart and mind are balanced by simple expressions of beauty around me. The sculptures my friend Mieke creates, the flowers my daughter brings me; these things are good and lovely and valuable. They help me.

As we begin to know God as an artist – *The* Artist – the obvious conclusion is that He is *the source of all creativity.* As we desire to grow in our own creative efforts, it makes sense that we draw on the Source and Originator of creativity to fill and flow in us. Our first step was to recognize Him as Artist, the source of creativity. Now we must move on, to recognize that if God loves creativity and wants fullness of life for us, He also wants to release creativity in each of us.

The fact that God has made each of us so uniquely different from one another is the first clue that God values the creative gifting in each of us. Truth be told, God placed it there. Scripture is full of the notion that God made us individually and by unique design. We are, after all, "fearfully and wonderfully made". We are "his workmanship, created in Christ Jesus for good works, which God prepared beforehand that we should walk in them" (Ephesians 2:10, NKJV). Further, we know He was carefully considering us as we were formed, for Jeremiah says (1:5), "Before I formed you in the womb I knew you, before you were born I set you apart." God was thinking of us, designing us, dreaming of us as we came into being. Each one is wonderfully made, created for good work and consecrated.

Our individual creative talent may not be in the traditional arts. It may be in computer science or economic genius. But creative it is, and God values it. God the Artist wants to bless and empower the creativity in each of us.

When I was a child, I was drawn to poetry. I would read and memorize poetry for the sheer pleasure of the beautiful words and the pictures they made for me in my mind. But somewhere along the line, I picked up the notion that being "artistic" like this wasn't a trait that would serve me well in life. Stability and common sense were the order of the day. Dreamy afternoons of poetry would not make me successful. Instead, they would leave me prone to an artist's temperament, and that, by all measures, would not be good. It wasn't until I was in my late thirties that I began to realize that I had shut something down in myself with this rejection of my nature.

When our son, Trevor, got his first guitar, I was witness to a transformation that began in him. A young man of only ten who struggled to put his feelings into words, he soon discovered that expression came easily through the music he began to write. His guitar was never far from him, and his personality calmed and matured as he unlocked himself with it.

One day, as he sat playing, I happened to be passing behind him. Without really planning to, I stopped and placed my hand on his head. I remember the way he turned to look over his shoulder at me, and his quizzical look asked me what I was doing.

"I'm blessing the music inside of you," I said simply.

I walked away… and he kept playing.

God is a far better parent than I am and my conviction today is that He wants to bless the creative in each of us. Artist God, who created a masterpiece of a world for us to live in and then made each of her inhabitants unique, wants to stir up and release your art. Be it in poetry or in sustainable development, music or environmental care, God's Spirit is longing to empower each one of us that we might be sources of beauty and blessing in this world.

Perhaps it's obvious to you already, but not all creativity expresses itself in what we think of as traditional art forms. The next time you reach up to replace a light bulb, take a moment to consider what a beautiful invention that delicate little glass ball is. To the beholder today, a light bulb is simply utilitarian. But think about the world it was invented in. Good lighting was a constant necessity for the quickly developing United States, yet oil-burning lamps were inefficient and dangerous. The sooty residue in homes and their propensity toward accidental explosions and injury made the available product of the times a risk factor that households simply had to endure. The need for a clean, safe answer for illumination was great, and while Edison doesn't get the sole credit for the first light bulb, he does carry the accolades for designing the first commercially practical bulb. The world has been better for it ever since. Yet even as I write, we need to move on to cleaner and more sustainable sources to light those bulbs. The need for creative development is ongoing.

Now imagine that God is willing – in fact eager – to touch your work with creativity and, through it, allow you to be a blessing. Maybe you work in human resources and the Spirit of God is hovering nearby with insight into bringing out the best in people. Maybe your work is in economics and the Spirit is standing by to stimulate new thinking in you that will change the way developing countries receive aid.

The God who made cocoa plants and taste buds and gave someone somewhere the ingenious notion to create the chocolate from those plants that so pleases our mouths is the very same God who is actively creating today. Let's partner with His creativity in and through us to bring all kinds of art and to make some beautiful differences in this world.

Responding to God as Artist and Source of Creativity

Make a date with God right now, or in the next few days, to listen to what He is saying through His handiwork. Give yourself at least an hour to be alone with Him in natural surroundings where you won't be disturbed. It could be as familiar as your favorite part of the back garden. It could be that you need to drive up into the hills, out into the countryside or to a lonely beach.

When you are comfortably situated, read the first two chapters of Genesis and think about the powerful creative energy resident in Artist God.

Now, quiet your heart and ask this simple question: "Creation, tell me about your Maker." Allow God's handiwork to bring you insights, no matter how small, into His character, His ways, His love.

Consider how you might have separated the art of creation from the Artist. How would keeping these two together change the way you see or care for the world around you? How would it change the way you experience God?

How does the notion that God made you individually and that He values your unique creative gifts affect the way you see yourself?

Think about the creative artist inside of you. If you were to name an area in which you have creativity, what would that be? Remember, it may not be in the traditional arts. It may be in medicine or water engineering or anything!

Thank God for His creative power and invite Him to flood your life with it. Invite God to release your unique gifts, that you might step deeper into who you are. Ask Him to stir up your creativity, that it might be a blessing.

God as Healer...

communion

crack open the disaster
the rich raw red flow of this soul

dark colors turning,
dancing in the night

breath!
it comes in gulps of
shattering cold

(breaking death)

crack open the disaster
the sheer shelter sham of self

tastes, heavy like dew,
pour together

life!
it comes surging
sure, strong

(unstoppable)

crack open the disaster

God as Healer

(Physician)

Standing on the narrow path, my husband, Byron, wondered what exactly to do next. He was walking through the open plains with a small group of Maasai men, but as they came around a bend in the trail the glossy black shimmer of a cobra reared up and hooded, just meters in front of them. He was thick and long and menacing in the heavy afternoon sun. Byron stopped, as you do!

Before he could even ponder the next move, a rush of air flew past him and the cobra was dead. Ole Nkomea had thrown his *orinka*, the traditional wooden club-like weapon that no self-respecting Maasai man would leave home without. Contrary to its non-aerodynamic-looking form, Maasai men can land their *orinka* with deadly accuracy.

During those years of living in remote regions of East Africa, carving the perfect *orinka* became kind of a hobby for Byron. Well, it became an obsession, really, if we're going to be honest. Soon my husband was well nigh an expert on all the factors that made for a good *orinka*, remembering where in the forest he saw an especially promising limb so he could return to it later with his axe.

One late afternoon, as he stood in the branches of a tree swinging the axe, the head of his tool came away from the handle, sailed in small circles through the air and landed neatly in the fleshy part of Byron's leg above his ankle. As our little family stood around the examination bed later, in the small medical clinic we administered, the boys watched with a gleeful kind of interest as their dad's leg was sewn safely closed.

But my mind went to other things. This wound of Byron's was easy to deal with. It was external, did not disturb any major arteries and was easy to clean and sew shut. *How easy it is at times to deal with external wounds. How very much harder it is to deal with the internal ones.* In fact, people had died at our clinic from internal wounds.

The hard truth of life is that we all have internal injuries. We may not have physical internal injuries, but we have injuries inside of us nonetheless. These injuries have stemmed from many things: events, words spoken to us, dreams that are broken, disappointments, losses and times of rejection. So many things in life can hurt us. And just like physical internal injuries, our internal wounds can be lethal. At the very least, they are toxic. They maim us in our ability to relate to God and stunt us in our capacity to relate to each other.

The question I'd like to consider, then, is whether or not God is a healer. Can we expect Him to be about our wholeness? Can He heal our internal wounds? Does He want us to know Him as a healer?

Looking into Scripture, I find that God is not just able to be our healer, but He desires to be this for us, as well. Consider these references:

He heals the brokenhearted
and binds up their wounds.

(Psalm 147:3)

The Lord is close to the brokenhearted
and saves those who are crushed in spirit.

(Psalm 34:18)

He has sent me [Jesus] to bind up the
brokenhearted...

(Isaiah 61:1)

I will be glad and rejoice in your love,
for you saw my affliction
and knew the anguish of my soul.

(Psalm 31:7)

As I read the Scriptures, the words "unfailing love" caught my attention.

May your unfailing love be my comfort...

(Psalm 119:76)

The Lord loves righteousness and justice;
the earth is full of his unfailing love.

(Psalm 33:5)

Let the morning bring me word of your unfailing
love,
for I have put my trust in you.

(Psalm 143:8)

God sees our suffering, and His love is unable to fail. I, on the other hand, have plenty of failing love in my life. I love my children passionately and care for them daily. I also fail them, most likely every day. I am unable to provide perfect or unfailing love, even with the enormity of what I feel for them. Yet this is not the case with God.

This is not even an exhaustive look at the Scriptures portraying God's heart that sees our pain and is willing and able to help us with it. When Scripture makes such a strong and recurring theme of something, we need to pay attention. Our pain and suffering is on God's mind. His desire to bring us into wholeness is ongoing, current and alive.

But how do we begin to know God as Healer? How do we begin to appropriate this aspect of His grace toward us?

Simplistic as it may sound, the starting point is belief. Do we believe what long lists of Scriptures report: that he is a compassionate God who sees our pain and moves to bind up our wounds? It may sound pathetically obvious, but believing that this is His character is where we must begin. Once we've established our footing on this foundation, we can take the next step.

I believe that the next step toward knowing God as Healer in my life is to begin to talk to Him about what's really going on inside of me. In the book of Job we read that Job's eyes "pour out tears" to God (16:20). The poet David frequently describes himself as pouring out his heart to God. The examples in Scripture of people who seemed to really be close to God describe, not surprisingly, people who opened up to him about how they really felt.

Now we may believe that we are talking to God openly and honestly. But often we're not. Stuck in our habits of keeping the hurts of our lives buried and hidden from those around us, we don't realize that we keep them away from God as well. By way of old patterns, we've learned to communicate in safe territory with this God who has so much grace and compassion for us.

This came into clear focus for me years ago, when our three boys were little. As much as I adored our three scraped-knees adventurers, something in my heart was longing for the presence of a little girl in our home. I wasn't disappointed in my children. No: I was proud of them and fiercely protective when anyone commented to me in their hearing that I must be less than completely thrilled that they were all male. This was outrageous to me. I loved my boys… I just wanted a little girl in my life as well.

But this very desire was my dilemma. How could I seriously go to God and tell him that I really wanted a baby girl? I mean *really now*! I had friends who hadn't been able to conceive and friends whose children were terribly ill. I had friends who had lost kids. And I was going to go to God and say, "Look, I know I have three perfectly healthy sons, but I need you to do one better for me, OK? I want a daughter and I'll be needing her to come along pretty quickly now, because I'm getting older – you know?"

Seriously, a prayer like that seemed severely out of line to me. And it would have been, if it had been smug or demanding. If there was even a trace of entitlement in there, it would have been an ugly little prayer. I was so afraid that my desire reflected some dissatisfaction with my boys or, worse, some ungrateful

attitude, that I would only touch quickly on my desire for a daughter. Almost like an add-on, I would say, "Oh, and could you see about this desire thing that I've got going on? If it would be your will," I would mumble hurriedly, "could we please have a baby girl?" Then I would move along to other things – briskly.

Yet this unfulfilled desire in my heart was like a little infected place that was beginning to fester and grow. It caused me pain, and one day, God just put His finger on it. As I prayed, I felt that God leaned in close and told me in no uncertain terms that I was not being vulnerable with Him. I was *not* being vulnerable in my conversations with Him. I was touching on a desire but not getting into the depth of it. I wasn't stepping out onto what I thought of as a thin edge and just exposing my heart and saying, "I *want* this! I just *want* a baby girl for no better reason than I simply *want* her and I feel like we're not all here in this family yet!"

Imagine that for a moment. Imagine the Most Loving Being Ever stepping up close and putting His finger on your chest and saying, "You are *not* being vulnerable with me, little one. You are *not* being real."

Honestly, this came as a shock to me. I thought I was being open in my prayer times, but clearly I was not. I was withholding. And the reason I was withholding was because I was afraid. If I exposed my heart and my desire to God and just got bare naked vulnerable with Him, what was I going to do if He didn't care? What if I put my desire out there and He ignored it, or told me that He had other plans? What if I stepped out on the thin edge and the answer was not what I wanted to hear? I was sure the edge would crumble beneath me and I didn't know where the fall would take me, but I was pretty certain it would hurt.

Faced with my own lack of vulnerability before God, I had to make a choice. I had to decide if I could trust His goodness. If the promise that He gives good gifts is true, was I able to trust that whatever the outcome was, that outcome would be His good gift? Maybe there would be no fourth baby. Maybe the fourth baby would be a fourth boy. Maybe the fourth baby would be a girl. Maybe the fourth baby would be healthy, but maybe not. Was I going to trust that His goodness would be present and primary in any of those results?

The point is that I needed to get real with God in order for Him to deal with some blockage in my heart toward Him. He wanted to heal my hurt, yes; but He also wanted to heal my ability to trust that He was good. He knew that this was a more fundamental hurt that needed to be dealt with first. I thought the issue was whether or not He would "allow" us a little girl. The issue that God saw – and wanted very much to heal – was my question regarding whether or not I could trust him with my desire; which is to say, would I trust him with my heart?

When I realized what was the real issue that we were dealing with, I understood why I danced so quickly over that part of my prayer. I was afraid for my heart, which is a fairly good reason to self-protect. But self-protection wasn't getting me any closer to authenticity in my relationship with God. I needed to decide if I trusted His goodness or not.

I stepped out onto that thin edge, explained my desire very clearly and then waited. I waited for a good year before this fourth baby was even conceived. I had lots of time to practice trusting His goodness in those long months. Then I waited two-thirds of the pregnancy before I found out that this fourth baby was in fact a girl. She arrived a healthy little girl and she is a delight. But God's goodness was already a real and solid bottom line to me long before she ever arrived.

I have no desire to concoct a formula to manipulate God into answering prayers the way we want them answered. I don't think that's possible, anyway. I just know that I had to get real with God before He could begin to answer my prayer, and the major hurdle to healing my hurt was not convincing Him to give me a baby girl, but deciding whether I could trust Him.

God deals directly and individually with us in our need for healing when we allow Him in like this. He also provides for our healing through community. We are created for relationship. God said that everything He created was good, but one of the first things He said about Adam was that it was *not* good that he be alone. We aren't meant to get through this life without one another. Ecclesiastes 4:9–11 tells us plainly that two are better than one because of the way that they help each other in life.

> *Two are better than one,*
> *because they have a good return for their labor:*
> *if they fall down,*
> *they can help each other up.*
> *But pity those who fall*
> *and have no one to help them up!*
> *Also, if two lie down together, they will keep warm.*
> *But how can one keep warm alone?*

God never expected us to be able to get through life without relationship. We are called to carry one another's burdens and celebrate one another's joys.

When I was eight years old, a teenage neighbor boy called me into his house and molested me. I knew immediately that I needed to talk to my parents about what had happened, but the confusion of feelings that I experienced because I was a child did not allow me to properly separate guilt, shame, horror, embarrassment and fear. In the immaturity of my mind, embarrassment and shame seemed to mean there must be some level of guilt on my part. Also, the feelings were just too raw to express very clearly. For whatever reason, I was able to give my parents only a sketchy portrayal of the event, keeping the worst of it to myself. And I carried it alone for years.

When I was thirteen, I had a best friend who was like a sister. We had found each other at age eleven, and we survived those awkward years of junior high in Southern California together. One late summer afternoon, I told Becky what had happened to me when I was eight. Now, seriously, what was another thirteen-year-old girl going to do to help the situation? Was she going to go find the guy thousands and thousands of miles away and beat him up? Was she going to explain maturely to me why there was no place for guilt or shame in my heart over this? Would she be able to erase the past?

No; all Becky could do was listen. Becky listened and felt badly with me… and a huge measure of healing came into my life. Over the next years, I was able to read a lot of helpful material on the subject and to talk about it with others, even revisiting it to some extent with my parents. But the biggest step forward in my healing came when I opened my thirteen-year-old heart and allowed a friend to carry the burden with me. *God brings us healing by giving us one another.*

It's important that I mention here that healing for sexual abuse (and many other emotional hurts) varies just as dramatically as the situations people experience. It would be negligent of me to leave the impression that sharing with a friend is all a person needs to do to find healing. My experience is that God used friendship and self-directed study to bring healing into my life; yet many friends of mine have found healing through counseling and specific prayer times. God infuses many approaches to healing and, I believe, brings His good results through many forms. Our job is not to tell Him in what manner our healing should come, but to expect Him to use the form He leads us into.

Scripture does not limit God's healing power to our internal ailments. Beyond binding up the broken-hearted and comforting those who are crushed in spirit, the Lord calls Himself the One who heals our physical illnesses as well. The poet David declares it clearly in Psalm 103:2–4:

> *Praise the Lord, my soul,*
> *and forget not all his benefits –*
> *who forgives all your sins*
> *and heals all your diseases,*
> *who redeems your life from the pit...*

But isn't it interesting that forgiveness of sin is listed, not as a precursor necessarily, but definitely something very important to be noted alongside? The psalm goes on, saying (verses 4–6):

... and [he] crowns you with love and compassion,
who satisfies your desires with good things
so that your youth is renewed like the eagle's.
The Lord works righteousness
and justice for all the oppressed.

This is a full-service type of healing that the Lord is into. He is willing and able to work toward a shalom sense of well-being in all the areas of our lives. And physical healing is part of that.

Historically, God's involvement (or seeming lack thereof) in physical healing has brought a lot of division in the Christian community. There are those at one end of the spectrum who firmly do not believe that God heals anyone miraculously today. Their conviction is that he uses doctors and medicine and our

proper self-care to bring about healing. There are those on the opposite end of the spectrum who believe that God will heal every snuffle or flu we have, if we only have the faith. And then there are people at every point of the spectrum in between.

Who is right? Don't I just wish I had the answer to that question!

Here's what I know: God is good and God is able. Here's what I don't know: when does it seem right to God to step in and heal miraculously? Why does He apparently do it at some times while not doing it at others? Those are the questions that I leave for academics and theologians to wrestle with. For me, I have to find a place to rest with this issue.

If it's true that the disciples would have known what the Father is doing by watching Jesus, then we have to admit that the Father must have been into healing our physical bodies, because Jesus did so much of that. Interestingly, though, Jesus often forgave sins along with physical healing. In Matthew 9:1–8 someone paralyzed is brought to Jesus. Jesus looks at him and says, "Don't worry; your sins are forgiven." He doesn't mention physical healing at all. It's not until the grumblers are overheard accusing Him of blasphemy because He assumed the role of God by forgiving sin that he actually speaks healing into the paralyzed person's body.

As with my experience long ago when I was longing for a daughter, Jesus saw the deeper thing that needed to be touched and He dealt with that first. Very possibly, He purposely delayed the physical healing just to give the doubters a lesson in who He was. They were appalled that He assumed God's role of forgiving sin, but He challenged them by saying, "Which is easier: to forgive the sin or to heal the body? Well, hey, guess what: I can do both."

In my own life I have experienced healing in many ways. I have experienced heart-healing – the healing of emotional hurts that were causing me to suffer. I've experienced physical healing through rest, as well as through better habits, therapy and medical intervention. I have marveled at the healing that comes "naturally", as bodies seem to know how to close wounds and grow new skin and bones know how to graft back together after they are set. I have also marveled at the in-breaking of God, when prayers have been spoken and healing has come right then and there. I have seen and experienced all these ways of healing in certain situations. In others, I have not. I have grieved when no amount of medical intervention or sincere prayer brought about the healing we all were looking to God for.

In regard to this issue, I have chosen to rest back in that place of believing in the goodness of God. Though I don't understand how He chooses when – or when not – to move miraculously on our behalf, I rest in the goodness I have come to know as true. I continue to pray and seek His healing touch in all manner of situations, and I'm sure that I always will. I trust Him to respond to those prayers from His goodness.

The final verses of Revelation speak to me on this. As the portrait of heaven unfolds, we see that there is a tree by the River of God. In what sounds almost like a simple, yet profound, editorial aside, the author says, "And the leaves of the tree are for the healing of the nations" (Revelation 22:2).

God's heart is for healing. I rest in the shade of that truth.

Responding to God as Healer

Make a date with God, right now or in the next few days. Again, clear enough space on your calendar to have a good, protected time with Him.

Before considering areas of your life in which you would like to experience healing, ask God to show you if there are places or issues in your life in which you are not being open and real with Him. How might these things be holding you back from intimacy in your relationship with God?

Focus your thoughts on one of these areas and ask yourself why you haven't been open or vulnerable with God about this.

Now consider Ephesians 3:17–19:

I pray that you, being rooted and established in love,
may have power, together with all the Lord's people,
to grasp how wide and long and high and deep is the
love of Christ, and to know this love that surpasses
knowledge – that you may be filled to the measure of
all the fullness of God.

What would it look like to invite God's love into the areas of hurt you have thought of? Take some time to do that now.

You may find that you have a small list accumulating of areas in your life that seem to need healing. Consider setting time aside weekly to invite God into each area, asking Him for direction on how to go forward in the healing process. Consider sharing these things with a trusted friend who would be willing to carry them with you.

There may be physical or emotional areas in your life that you have sought healing for before, but have seen no change. How might disappointment with God be affecting your relationship with Him?

Allow yourself the freedom to express this disappointment to God. Be honest with Him.

What would trusting God's goodness mean for these situations? Consider releasing each area to His goodness. Spend some time journaling the choice to trust His goodness.

Re-read the passage from Ephesians.

> *I pray that you, being rooted and established in love, may have power, together with all the Lord's people, to grasp how wide and long and high and deep is the love of Christ, and to know this love that surpasses knowledge — that you may be filled to the measure of all the fullness of God.*

God as Guide...

pruning

you come pruning
and i expect
the cutter's blade
biting into my flesh
to sever the ugly
deadness

but you come pruning
with gifts of love
so much bigger than
my arms can hold

and i
embarrassed by the
wide expanse of
your love
bow down
breaking off these dry branches
that you might
carry them
away

(Director)

It wasn't turning out anything like what we had expected. We were very young, newly arrived in East Africa, our hearts filled with ideas of service to the underprivileged and forgotten. We had been so excited to finally get here, now that I had finished my degree and we had successfully navigated our first two years of marriage. Byron had completed his degree earlier and had spent these last two years in preparation, earning our keep but also gaining as many practical skills as possible. Finally, we were in Kenya, ready to head north and assume leadership of a project that would involve introducing appropriate development and technology while overseeing a sponsorship program for school-age children.

But now that we were physically present and ready to report to the project, we were confused to find that there really was no way for us to go forward with it. The national office of the organization we were volunteering with was in crisis. The directors had just resigned, having run the programs into debt and disarray. The vehicle that was supposed to be allocated for us to take north was not in running order and there was no money to get it repaired. All the accounts were depleted and the national staff was deeply discouraged. The new director was a sincere and honest man with a great heart and he would have loved to have things running smoothly. It was just that there weren't two shillings to rub together in this sad little shell of an organization.

As for us, we were somewhat dumbfounded. How could things be so different from what we had imagined? How had this become the culmination of our preparation, fundraising and strong desire to give ourselves on behalf of others? As far as we could see, this was just one giant mess – not to mention a huge disappointment. We were stuck in Nairobi, living in a grungy little apartment, spending our days mostly doing nothing at a dimly lit office of depressed activists.

Our prayers went something like this: "Um – hello, God. Are you there?"

Enter some older folks. What an unbelievable resource of wisdom and encouragement it was for us when a couple in their late forties and another couple in their early seventies reached out to us. Over meals and multiple cups of tea, through conversation and prayer together, these friends helped us sort through our options and plan the way ahead.

Proverbs 16:9 says: "In their hearts human beings plan their course, but the Lord establishes their steps." As is so often the case with hindsight, we have an entirely different understanding of this time of frustration in Nairobi now, with the passage of the years. What came out of that disappointing landing in Kenya was an internship that would change our lives. Taking us in a different direction from what we had originally planned for, the following two years exposed us to opportunities and growth that were not a part of the work we had originally come to do. What we became involved with instead had less to do with physical help and more to do with spiritual growth in the personal lives of young, educated Africans, who had the potential to take positions of leadership in the years ahead. It was an entirely different way of giving assistance to Africa, as it touched on character and the practical outworkings of faith on a continent so desperately in need of leaders with deep-rooted integrity.

We look back on those days hoping that the students we worked among experienced lasting growth. We know that *we* did. The last-minute change of plan was a door for us that led into our own personal development and the discovery of things that were deeply embedded in our hearts. It was during this "unplanned" internship that we first realized how much we love to see people grow in authentic, practical, living relationship with their Maker. Combining this important element with our desire to make a physical difference in the challenging lives so many Africans face has been key to shaping all our years since then. What's more, we

couldn't have applied for this internship from the United States. This was an invitation-only opportunity that opened because we were already in the country. We had planned our course. The Lord had directed our steps.

God as Guide… God as Director. What if we actually invited God to show us how to navigate the practical as well as what we think of as the spiritual aspects of life? What would it mean to allow God into daily decisions and choices?

The first qualities in a director or guide are that this person be available, have wisdom and have our best interest at heart. The questions to be asked are: "Will this person be good for me and, if so, is there a willingness to engage in my life?" Considering these things as they apply to God might feel a little odd, or hard to get at. Yet I believe that we have to settle them as the starting point. There is no real help in a mentoring-type friendship if

I constantly second-guess the trustworthiness of the advice or instruction I'm receiving. If I don't have confidence in the model being lived before me, there isn't much point in looking at a person's life as a guide for my own. And even if the person is wise and worth emulating, there's not much point to seeking them out if they aren't interested in being involved in me.

By even the most basic definition of what it means to be divine, we have to recognize that God is fundamentally wise. In one of my favorite passages of Scripture, God describes Himself to the Old Testament man Job. Job has endured terrible suffering, and his friends have been offering spectacularly unhelpful advice regarding the reasons for – as well as suggested responses to – these trials.

Finally, God seems to have had enough of all the babbling. Taking well over two thousand words, God describes Himself to Job in strong, clear language. In chapters 38–42 of Job, we find some of the most awe-inspiring text ever written. Here, in a list of questions and declarations, the Maker of the universe asks Job if he has any of the knowledge, power or wisdom that He, Himself, carries within. He is asking Job if he, based on all this history, has any right to stand there, questioning God's ways.

Foundational to all, then, there is unfathomable wisdom residing in the heart of God. We can trust that God has what is required to be a good guide. But *will He* guide us, or is He more of a remote overseer?

Once again, I am inspired by David's life and how he related to God as his Guide. Psalm 16 speaks of the direction that David receives from God. Verse 7 says, "I will praise the Lord, who counsels me; even at night my heart instructs me."

First of all, David is experiencing counsel from the Lord. He refers to it as a fact: a practical help that comes any time he is in need. In the peace of the night his heart is used by God to give him instruction. I've experienced this as well! Maybe David was like me, with too much going on around him during the day to hear the Lord very clearly. Come to think of it, he must have had it far worse than I do. What with wars to fight and giants to kill, a disturbed king who was bent on killing him, the trouble with that little issue of falling for his neighbor's wife, and a nation to lead, his life was an endless march of complications to drive him to distraction.

Yet God counseled him. The Lord spoke through his heart at night. Though his issues may have been a little more complex at times than my everyday struggles, his guidance came, as mine often does, in the quiet hours when the household is sleeping. Many times I have awoken in the night and seen a clear, new direction to take on a puzzling matter. It's as if I can't hear the Lord in the noisy hullabaloo of my day, so He waits patiently to instruct me in the night. "Wake up, Lisa. I have an idea for you." I have so often received insight this way, and it sounds as if David experienced this as well.

Because of this, I've learned to expect God and invite Him to guide me in the night. Of course, I'm happy for Him to lead me at any time, but I have very often climbed into bed perplexed about something and simply asked the Lord to speak to me in the next few hours, as I sign off for the day. "Feel free to wake me up with some counsel, Lord," I'll say. Sometimes I get the middle-of-the-night session with him. Other times, I've woken up thinking more clearly, an answer dawning on me as the sun lifts up over the horizon.

This willingness of God to meet us and bring counsel is confirmed in the book of James. James 1:5 says:

If any of you lacks wisdom, you should ask God, who gives generously to all without finding fault, and it will be given to you.

James doesn't say, "and it *might* be given to you"; he doesn't say, "and God will lay out some impossibly veiled clues and you'll have to guess your way forward." No; James says God gives the wisdom generously and without finding fault. Wow, this is the kind of wisdom-giver we need! He isn't tearing off a stingy scrap of wisdom that won't take us far. Nor does he size up our worthiness before doling it out. Instead, God generously bestows the wisdom we need, even when we are full of weakness and fault.

Why is God so ready to guide us? I think the simple answer is that He loves us. He cares about how life goes for us. He has our best interest in mind. His hope for us is that we will have peace and joy in the here and now of daily life. Contrary to the popularized notion that God is a grumpy rule-maker, God gives wisdom and direction because He wants us to be happy.

David understood this relationship between choosing to look to God and the joy that follows. We looked at Psalm 16 and saw that David was praising God for counseling him, affirming that the Lord speaks to him in the night. He then goes on (16:8),

> *I keep my eyes always on the Lord.*
> *With him at my right hand, I will not be shaken.*

David has made the choice to keep his eyes on the Lord; to place Him always before him. He is living in close connection with God, heeding the instruction he receives, dwelling near Him. And this, he knows, brings the security of not being shaken. Yet this is not the only result. Taking it further (16:9), he says,

> *Therefore my heart is glad and my tongue rejoices...*

Listening to the wisdom and instruction of God brings David joy. In the beautiful, affirming conclusion of this psalm (16:11, TNIV), David makes big, broad statements:

You make known to me the path of life;
you will fill me with joy in your presence,
with eternal pleasure at your right hand.

David is saying that God has directed him on the path of life. God has nudged and guided, granted wisdom and given instruction all along the way, and this has led to the best path for David's life. Following this path has meant the felt presence of God with him in the journey. This presence produces joy in David and, as he follows closely, he experiences lasting pleasure.

In sharp contrast to this, earlier in the psalm David says that following anyone other than God will only bring people problems (16:4, TNIV): "Those who run after other gods will suffer more and more." It's just not worth it, he's saying. Setting someone or something other than God before you as your guiding goal simply ends up increasing the struggles of life.

But how do we practically seek the guidance, wisdom and direction of God? How do we begin to live with Him as our Life Coach? I believe it begins with simple obedience to what we know God is saying. Jesus boiled the essence of following God

down into two commands that cover quite a lot. When asked what the greatest, or most important commandment was, he drew from the Old Testament and then added to it. Matthew 22:37–39 says:

> *"Love the Lord your God with all your heart and*
> *with all your soul and with all your mind.""This is*
> *the first and greatest commandment. And the second*
> *is like it: "Love your neighbor as yourself."*

The first steps of obedience then are about love. To love God with all of my heart and soul is a pretty big goal, and I don't think it's something I can simply decide to do from here on out. Instead, it's the daily choices I make in the small things to put God first in my heart and in my soul. To "put Him first in my heart" means, I think, to consider His ways and apply them in my daily life. As I make these choices, I actively love Him.

Perhaps the most basic starting point is to consider the spiritual fruit that Paul speaks of in Galatians. Early in chapter 5 (verse 6), he makes the strong statement that "The only thing that counts is faith expressing itself through love" (whoa!). He goes on to say that we are called to be free, reflecting again that God is not a rule-maker. And with this freedom, we are not to simply indulge ourselves in whatever pursuit we feel like getting into, but to serve each other in love. Paul goes back to Jesus' words, telling the Galatians that the whole of the law is summarized in this one thing: that we are to love our neighbors as ourselves. Now, as this chapter draws to a close, he speaks of what this might look like, as he points out the fruit that is a result of welcoming God's Spirit to live in us. Verses 22–23 list these for us:

> *But the fruit of the Spirit is love, joy, peace, patience, kindness, goodness, faithfulness, gentleness and self-control. Against such things there is no law.*

We need to read these verses slowly and meditate on them. The problem is that we hear these nouns in our heads like a trite Sunday-school list for little girls in patent-leather shoes. Kindness!

Goodness! How do these fit into the competitive workplace of the twenty-first century? What do those things look like in the "real" world? It's easy to dismiss the list and miss its call to a subversively lived life. But don't let's miss it!

Imagine putting love into practice. Imagine inviting God's Spirit more and more deeply into your life and experiencing the depth of His love for you. Now imagine that love breaching the boundaries of your heart and spilling out to the people in your life. This kind of love is both an outcome and a choice. We experience it as it fills us, and it can't help but spill over. But there will probably still be many times in every day when we have to choose it. Responding with love to those who behave lovingly toward us isn't actually hard. Responding with love to those who are not behaving lovingly toward us… well, that's a different thing. Yet, as we draw on the Spirit's power within us and make the choice to love, it can happen.

And what about the other fruits of the Spirit? Consider joy, peace, patience, kindness, goodness, faithfulness, gentleness and self-control. Just like love, each one can come forth as a result of the Spirit dwelling in us and from the choices the Spirit helps us to make. The presence of God's Spirit in us stimulates and grows these characteristics, while our choices to live them strengthen and mature them within us. Each one is counter to what we might consider "normal" human reactions in challenging relationships, discouraging circumstances and impossible scenarios. But as they are chosen and embraced, they are powerful to effect change in and around us.

With every choice to live these qualities, we embrace God's ways and live our love for Him. With every choice to love Him and live His ways, we put Him first in our hearts and welcome Him to be our Guide.

But the command also says to love God with our minds and with our strength. Loving God with our mind implies intelligent contemplation of Him. There is an expectation that knowing, following and loving Him will excite our thinking and encourage further study and meditation. More romantically, as we begin to know God better, we'll find that we're thinking about Him more. Loving God means that He is on our minds. And the more He is on our minds and we choose to follow His way, the more easily we learn to recognize His promptings and guidance. Growth in our mentorship under Him happens as we love Him, listen to Him and live out what we're hearing.

Living it out is part of the practical application of the second part of what Jesus said about the greatest commandment. We are asked to love our neighbors as we love ourselves. The wonderful and often-overlooked clause in this part of the command implies that we need to love ourselves. This ability to love ourselves is the base from which we're able to love others. Meditating on God's many ways of loving us, the way He fathers and mothers and befriends us, prepares us to understand that we are loved.

Receiving His release of creativity into our lives and work, His healing into our hearts and bodies and His guidance on the journey teaches us that we are worth His time and attention for perhaps no other reason than He wants to give us His time and attention. Pondering this huge God-love toward us begins to cancel the lies that some of us carry that say we aren't loveable and therefore cannot love ourselves.

Now, from this place of knowing we are loved, we are freed to love and care for ourselves and to allow this healthy state of being to pour out as love for our neighbors, near and far. In this way, looking to God as our Guide leads us into health and releases His love into the world.

Allowing God to be our Guide, then, begins with those small steps of obedience to what we learn through the written message of God in the Bible and what we hear His Spirit prompting in our heart. Yet even more basic than these is the simple foundational truth that God *is* the shepherd we need as we navigate this life.

Easily the best-recognized psalm the world over, Psalm 23 tells us in six declarative verses that God is a loving, skilled, able and willing Guide.

- He is the shepherd who provides, so that we are not lacking.

- He directs us into restful places, so that our souls are refreshed on the way.

- He shows us how to make good choices and live in a way that honors who He is.

- Even when we're in dark places of fear and death, we won't be overcome by that fear, or the evil that presses in, because His presence and His guidance comfort and encourage us.

- He provides for us abundantly and in a celebratory way, in plain view of our adversaries, who witness that He honors and blesses us.

- He sends His goodness and love to follow us all through life and welcomes us to remain with Him for ever.

David, who looked after sheep long before he looked after nations, recognizes the Shepherd heart of God because he knows the character and skill of a good shepherd. Seeing these qualities in God, he allows himself to be led.

And yet this wise, skilled Shepherd God leads us gently. There is no bullying in God's way. Isaiah 40:11 says:

He tends his flock like a shepherd:
He gathers the lambs in his arms
and carries them close to his heart;
he gently leads those that have young.

This is a compassionate leader who tends to the needs of his flock, not forgetting the extra care needed by the weakest ones. He understands the condition that each one is in and He assists each of us with patience. I feel this patience from the Lord. I believe God beckons me toward growth through the circumstances of life that I find myself in. Yet He does it with tremendous patience. When our two older boys left at the end of the summer a couple of years ago, I found myself longing to be able to keep the day from happening. In bed that morning I squeezed my eyes closed and asked my husband if he thought we could hold the day back by refusing to open our eyes. He shut his eyes with me, but we knew the minutes were still ticking on.

That afternoon, we put the boys on the shuttle to Nairobi, the first leg of a forty-two-hour journey back to their lives as students in California. Byron, Colin, Heather and I stood frozen to our spots in the parking lot after the bus pulled away, hot tears streaming down our faces.

In the next few achy days (and weeks!) I knew I had a choice. I could nurse my hurt or give place to my healing. There was nothing wrong with hurting over their departure, but I didn't want to settle into that pain like a long-term tenant. The boys were growing up, and that was delightful to see. And I had the clear impression that there was growth for me in the whole process, as well.

Yet, in it all, I felt only the compassionate care of the Lord. Though I could sense His invitation to grow through it, I clearly felt Him allowing me to move at my own pace. Just like Isaiah's shepherd who lifts the lambs to carry them close to his heart and gently leads those who have young, I could feel the Lord adjusting His gait and slowing to a stop, allowing me all the time I needed to grieve. "This," I thought, "is the tenderness of the Lord." He never rushes on into growth.

Finally, this Shepherd Guide waits to be invited. As I said before, God does not bully us into allowing Him to become our Director and Instructor. In Psalm 25:4–5, David extends this invitation to the Lord:

> *Show me your ways, Lord,*
> *teach me your paths.*

Guide me in your truth and teach me,
for you are God my Savior,
and my hope is in you all day long.

Recognizing that God is wise and endlessly available, David opens his life continuously to God's guiding input. Then, as if to emphasize again the truth that God *desires* to guide us, the Psalm continues by saying that the Lord *instructs [us] in his ways* (8), *guides the humble* (9) and *confides in those who fear him* (14). Yes, this God is a willing coach, who will take us forward into life as we invite Him to do so.

Responding to God as Guide

Make a date with God, either right now or in the next few days. As always, leave yourself enough undistracted time to get the most out of this date with Him.

As you begin, take a few minutes to think about people who have been helpful guides or mentors on your personal journey. Think about how it felt to have their input in your life.

Spend a few minutes thinking about the different ways they helped guide you, then thank God for His provision of those people at different times in your life. You may want to thank them as well.

When we make the "little" decisions to obey what we hear God saying in His Word and by His Spirit, we put Him first in our hearts and this allows Him to lead us more easily. Take some time to listen for any promptings from God that you may have been missing in the busyness of life. Journal a bit about what you seem to hear from God on this.

Look at the list of Spiritual fruit from Galatians 5: love, joy, peace, patience, kindness, goodness, faithfulness, gentleness and self-control. Are there some of these that you feel better about or stronger in lately? Which of them stand out as areas that you would really like the Spirit to help you grow in?

Read Psalm 23 through several times, meditating a little on each verse. Reflect on times in your life when you felt the Lord guiding and shepherding you.

Now rewrite this psalm in your own words. Take the time to do this thoughtfully. You might find that putting it into your own words will help you see ways in which the Lord has gently led, cared and provided for you.

Friend, Father, Mother, Artist, Healer, Guide

In these six essays we've looked at God as Friend, Father, Mother, Artist, Healer and Guide. Looking back, is there one of these that stands out as your most comfortable or common way of knowing or understanding God? Take some time thinking about how this connection with God developed.

Take a few minutes to meditate on each of these six areas. Ask the Lord to point out which one or two He would like to explore further with you at this time in your life.

Write a letter to God inviting Him to take you into a closer relationship with Him. Dream with Him about how you'd like to know Him.

Take some time now to simply linger and enjoy God.